THE MONTESSORI MANUAL

Maria Montessori was born in 1870, and she was the first woman ever granted a medical degree by an Italian university. As a child, she showed great ability in mathematics and originally intended to become an engineer. She did postgraduate work in psychiatry.

At the age of 28, Montessori became directress of a tax-supported school for defective children. Working thirteen hours a day *with the children*, she developed materials and methods which allowed them to perform reasonably well on school problems previously considered far beyond their capacity. Her great triumph, in reality and in the newspapers, came when she presented children from mental institutions at the public examinations for primary certificates, which was as far as the average Italian ever went in formal education — and her children passed the exam.

Typically, she drew from her experience the vigorous conclusion — that if *these* children could be brought to the academic levels reached by normal children, then there had to be something horribly wrong with the education of normal children. And so she moved on to the *normal* children of the slums. Thereafter, by her own desire and by public demand, she was an educator, not a medical doctor.

Montessori's insights and methods are contained in four basic texts, now republished: THE MONTESSORI METHOD, SPONTANEOUS ACTIVITY IN EDUCATION (*The Advanced Montessori Method*, volume 1), THE MONTESSORI ELEMENTARY MATERIAL (*The Advanced Montessori Method*, volume 2), and DR. MONTESSORI'S OWN HANDBOOK.

THE MONTESSORI METHOD, by Maria Montessori. Introduction by Martin Mayer. The education of children from 3 to 6. With all the original photographs. 50 photos/figures. 448 pages. $6.50

SPONTANEOUS ACTIVITY IN EDUCATION, by Maria Montessori. *The Advanced Montessori Method*, volume 1. The education of children from 7 to 11. 384 pages. $6.50

THE MONTESSORI ELEMENTARY MATERIAL, by Maria Montessori. *The Advanced Montessori Method*, volume 2. The education of children from 7 to 11. 116 photos/figures. 512 pages. $8.50

DR. MONTESSORI'S OWN HANDBOOK, by Maria Montessori. 43 photos/figures plus 1 four-color photo. 170 pages. $5.00

MONTESSORI FOR PARENTS, by Dorothy Canfield Fisher. 20 photos plus 1 four-color photo. 288 pages. $5.95

THE MONTESSORI MANUAL FOR TEACHERS AND PARENTS, by Dorothy Canfield Fisher. Practical exercises and lessons on the use of the apparatus in homes and schools, nature study, and an extended discussion on Montessori discipline and obedience. 15 photos plus 1 four-color photo. 154 pages. $5.00

NEW EDITIONS PUBLISHED BY
ROBERT BENTLEY, INC.
18 Pleasant St., Cambridge, Massachusetts 02139

Dr. Montessori

THE
MONTESSORI MANUAL

For Teachers and Parents

BY

DOROTHY CANFIELD FISHER

WITH SIXTEEN PHOTOGRAPHS,
ONE IN FOUR COLORS

1964
ROBERT BENTLEY, INC.
18 PLEASANT ST., CAMBRIDGE, MASSACHUSETTS 02139

FOREWORD

It is now a year since the publication of "The Montessori Mother," a year which has brought to the author of that volume a great mass of correspondence and innumerable personal interviews with American mothers interested in the new ideas about the education of young children. This first-hand experience with a wide circle of searchers for information has shown me the need, in the case of mothers untrained in educational methods, of a more concrete and definite and less philosophical presentation of the ideas of the great Italian teacher.

This unpretentious Manual is designed to meet that need and to be used by mothers of young children.

It is also hoped that teachers will receive valuable hints from the suggestions in its pages, which their greater experience and professional training will enable them to expand into school-room exercises. For instance, many of the games and all of the gymnastic exercises suggested are practicable and desirable for any playground where young children gather.

As a majority of the letters received from inquiring mothers have been concerned with the prickly questions of obedience and the general disciplinary atmosphere of the young child's life, I have thought best to add to the remarks about the use of the manufactured and home-made apparatus, some practical hints about the disciplinary management of young children. It is my earnest hope that these suggestions as to the daily routine of life for young children will aid some of the mothers perplexed about the problem of teaching their children the habit of cheerful, sunny self-discipline and self-control.

DOROTHY CANFIELD FISHER.

Arlington, Vermont, August, 1913.

TABLE OF CONTENTS

ILLUSTRATIONS

REPRESENTATIVE PARTS OF THE MONTESSORI DIDACTIC APPARATUS

(Opposite Page 30)

THE MONTESSORI MANUAL

I

SOMETHING WRONG WITH MODERN EDUCATION

One of the most distinguishing features of twentieth-century life is the deep-rooted, wide-spread dissatisfaction with the way modern children are being educated. In most great world-centers one finds the same naïve certainty that there, in that spot, the problem is most insoluble, and that elsewhere conditions are better. In our America everyone is decrying our national fault of cheap superficiality as the poison of our schools and looking with longing eyes toward the "thoroughness" of German and English methods. In England they are bewailing their hide-bound, slow conservatism and envying American flexibility and quickness in facing the problem of education. In France they are appalled at the mental inertia of the pupils and in Germany they are crying out that their insistence on the letter has killed the spirit.

The truth seems to be that we are suddenly demanding more of education than we ever before dreamed possible. It is not that our schools or our methods of education are worse than those which have preceded them, but that we see them to be so far, far below what they might be—what they ought to be. The disquieting truth which has so upset us all is that there is no real reason why every child should not be really educated in the way which would bring out the greatest number possible of his own individual powers, which are, of course, different from the powers of every other human being in the world.

We are all dolefully agreed that this is not being done, that a large per cent of the innate abilities of the population of the world is wasted for lack of proper training, and that a tragic per cent of the time spent in school, is spent to no purpose, is practically blotted from the all-too-short lives of the helpless children, subjected to a meaningless routine.

A highly successful head of a department in a New York Public High School told me, not long ago, that after his lifetime of experience in modern education he had sickening moments of doubt as to whether the whole system did not do more harm than good, inasmuch as it seemed to crush out what small natural, genuine *living* abilities the children have, in order to replace these by a certain amount of rote-learned "information." "We destroy," he said, sadly, "the living, vital, eternal and immortal processes of invention, resourcefulness and logic and prop up unsteadily in their places, a large number of facts, which will all be swept away by the research of the next fifty years."

This note of alarm is to be heard from every corner of the civilized world, clear, unmistakable, practically unanimous.   But the chorus of suggested causes for this lamentable condition is confusing in its variety; while as for possible remedies, the contradictory recommendations are deafening and innumerable.

TIME UNPROFITABLY SPENT.—And yet there are one or two common notes, one or two commonly admitted flaws in present systems of education. Everywhere people cry out that children do not make the most of their time; that only a small part of their school-life is spent in educating themselves; that most of it seems to be spent unprofitably, for one reason or another, mostly for reasons connected with our traditional ideals of school order and discipline and regularity.   And yet these ideals are, in spite of all the uneasiness, usually accepted unquestioningly, as though they were axiomatic laws of nature.   We are told that

with modern conditions, there cannot be, at the
very least, less than thirty children in a class;
which means with present school methods that during a great deal of the time, twenty-nine children
are sitting passively, waiting their turn, while one
child is getting a little brief educational exercise;
which means that lessons must be kept down to
the capacity of the dullest of the thirty and,
therefore, that twenty-nine children, finishing their
lesson before him, must pass empty, profitless time,
varying in a vicious ratio according to their
native ability.

THE BRIGHT CHILD UNPROVIDED FOR BY PRESENT
SYSTEM.—Everyone must remember the pregnant
exclamation of the old educator at the great educational convention, "We have methods for the
dull child, and systems for the deficient child, but
God help the bright child!"

To keep thirty children moving as one, which
is (so we seem to think) the only way to avoid
intellectual and moral anarchy and chaos, a great
deal of avowed and a still greater deal of un-
avowed marking-time is necessary. One boy has
a natural gift for mathematics, and in two months
time has mastered the arithmetical work intended
for the year in his class. Is his mind given more
of the food it craves and which it can so well
digest? Is he allowed to go on, to take the next

step for which he is so eagerly ready? Not at all. His memory is not quick to retain the insanities of English spelling, and hence, so goes our logic, he must wait a year before he is allowed to go forward in mathematics. He must waste a year of his short life—it is even worse than wasted, for the continual reiteration in daily recitations of problems which he has already mastered, dull the natural keenness of his mind and sicken him of the whole subject; so that when he is finally allowed to advance, he has but a listless attention for what, ten months before, would have been an intellectual feast for an eager appetite.

ARBITRARY CLASSIFICATION UNDESIRABLE.—Our educational specialists admit that this is unfortunate, but insist that it is inevitable. What can be done? A big schoolhouse, containing six hundred children, would be, we are told, in utter confusion and turmoil if the children were allowed continually to pass from one class to another. Who would decide every day or even every week which class each child belonged to? As if it made the slightest difference what class a child belongs to, if he is being satisfactorily educated! It seems incredible to us now that in the eighteenth century when Braddock's soldiers went marching out to fight the Indians, that no one thought of asking, "What is the good of all those fine red coats, if the soldiers only fight the worse because of them?" Possibly in the twenty-first century it will seem incredible that none of us asked, "What is the good of classifying children arbitrarily if they only learn the worse because of it?" Those ordered phalanxes, marching up and down our well-ordered schoolhouse halls, are all very well; but have they anything to do with educating the individual child—and, of course, the individual child is all we ever have to educate.

CHILDREN BECOME PASSIVE.—In the chorus of complaint of our systems of education, I detect another note common to all countries and all temperaments. Somehow, we accuse ourselves, we have mismanaged things so that children in the schoolroom have a strange tradition of passivity, instead of their natural buoyant impulse to action, so noticeable on their playgrounds. As one teacher cried out to me not long ago in a fit of exasperation, "By the time they reach me they haven't enough intellectual curiosity left to save their minds alive! Do what I will, all *they* do is to sit back and watch me teach." In our reaction from the piercing intellectual bleakness of the Puritan régime of *force* in education, we seem to have created in our schoolrooms an enervating atmosphere in which there is but little brisk, tonic invitation to keep moving intellectually. The child

At undirected play with the didactic or sense-training materials

who sits passively quiet is too often praised as being a "good" child. He is too often encouraged to do this instead of to exercise his intellectual muscles by a constant participation in a variety of interesting movements, taken spontaneously.

II

DR. MONTESSORI TO THE RESCUE—THE UNDERLYING IDEA OF HER SYSTEM

It was with the echo in my ears of a great deal of such clamor and unrest from both teachers and parents that I went to Rome the winter of 1911-1912, having for one of my objects the investigation of a new system of education for very small children, said to have been devised by an Italian woman. I was in rather a sceptical frame of mind. There have been in America a good many new "systems" of education which have come to very little. Italy is notoriously behind the rest of the world in her public schools. It seemed not likely that America would have much to learn from a new variety of Kindergarten established in Rome. Before I went to visit this new variety of infant-school, I procured the book written on the system by the woman-doctor who had founded it. I found the volume in some ways rather hard reading, written in difficult Italian, full of technical terms, medical facts of which I had been ignorant, physiological pyschology and the nervous reactions in the human brain. But in spite of all these difficulties I was held as I have never been held by the most absorbing novel, and when I finally laid down the bulky volume, it was with the certainty of having seen a great light.

Here was a doctor, who had begun with a purely medical interest in children's brains, who had grappled hand to hand with the heart-breaking problem of the education of mentally deficient children and who, in that struggle, had discovered certain laws about the intellectual tendencies and intellectual activities of childhood in general. She "discovered" them, as a scientist does discover general laws, as Newton discovered the law of gravity. He was not the first man who had ever seen an apple drop to the ground. Everybody for centuries had known that they fall thus, and had been taking advantage in a fitful, irregular way of this only half-consciously known information. Newton "discovered" no new thing. He formulated the general underlying principles, involved in phenomena already observed, he made that information accurate, definite, to be counted upon, to be employed with certainty of the result, to be used, as it has been used, in the exploration of the solar system.

Dr. Montessori emerged from her laboratory work with deficient children with scientific proofs of certain fundamental principles of children's intellectual processes. And, being a scientist, she did what few of us really can do, she believed in facts scientifically proved.

ACTS UPON FACTS SCIENTIFICALLY PROVED.— What were these facts? In essence nothing new, nothing that we do not admit in theory, although we do not have the courage to act upon them. What is so startling about Dr. Montessori's attitude towards education is the honest, scientist's integrity of her logic. She continually says, in substance, "If that is the way children are made, our business is to educate them accordingly."

One of the facts she rediscovered is the old threadbare truism that every child is different from every other child. We all knew that before. The only difference between Dr. Montessori and the rest of us is that we disregard this well-known factor in the problem and that she takes it fully into account. It is not surprising that she does her educational sum with much more nearly an approximation to the right answer, than our wildly varying and always highly inaccurate results.

Dr. Montessori found that not only does every child differ from every other child but, not being a fixed and inanimate object, he is in a constant state of flux, and differs from himself, from day to day, as he grows. His attention, his memory, his mental endurance, his intellectual interest and curiosity, are not only unlike those of the child next him in school, but will be tomorrow different from what they are today. Then instead of turning tail and running away (as most of our educators do) from the tremendous problem involved in adequately treating such complicated little organisms, Dr. Montessori faced the situation squarely, accepting as every scientist does, the odds given him by Mother Nature. It was evident to her that the usual "class recitation" and "class lessons" were out of the question, since they could at the best, possibly fit the needs of only one child in the class. And yet it is obviously impossible, as the world is made up, to have a teacher for every child. There was only one way out—things must somehow be so organized and arranged that, for most of the time, the child can and shall teach himself.

THE UNDERLYING IDEA.—And here Dr. Montessori found herself in happy accord with another fundamental principle of the growth of childhood, which she had discovered or rediscovered and which may be said broadly to be *the* master idea of her system. The central idea of the Montessori system, on which every smallest bit of apparatus, every *detail of technic rests solidly, is a full recog-*

*nition of the fact that no human being is educated
by anyone else. He must do it himself or it is
never done.* The learner must do his own learning, and this granted, it follows naturally that the
less he is interfered with by arbitrary restraint
and vexatious, unnecessary rules, the more quickly,
easily and spontaneously he will learn. Everyone
who wishes to adopt her system, or to train children according to her method, must learn constantly to repeat to himself and to act upon, at
every moment, this maxim, "All growth must come
from a VOLUNTARY action of the child HIMSELF."

THE SYSTEM MUST FIT THE CHILD.—In this
respect again Dr. Montessori took squarely the
stand that education must be made to fit the child
and the child not forced to fit a preconceived idea
of what education ought to be or do. She laid
down in the first place the principle that one of
the essentials of education is that children shall
get that individual attention they need so much,
by giving it to themselves, each child being his own
teacher. She now further stated as another essential element that education should be so organized
that the child shall ardently desire to teach himself and shall enjoy doing it more than anything
else.

To reduce then, to the barest outline (because
that is the most easily grasped and retained), this

Children busy with the Cylindrical
Insets

The Dressing Frames are fascinating
for small children

Learning Muscular Co-ordination by
means of the Metal Insets

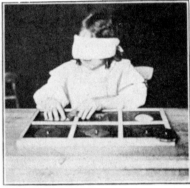

The Blindfold Game with the Wooden
Insets—Developing the Muscular
Sense

new system of training children, one can say that it rests upon a full conviction of these three facts about the nature of children:

First.—Children are all different from each other, and hence need for their fullest development, the greatest possible liberty for their individualities to grow; and that, though of course there are many points in common, they must not be treated in the lump, but individually.

Second.—Children cannot, so to speak, learn from the outside. That is, that the impulse to learn *must* come from within their own minds. There are absolutely no exceptions to this rule. Children must wish to learn, or it is a physical impossibility for them to do so.

Third.—Children are so made that, *given proper conditions,* they prefer educating themselves to any other occupation.

III

AN ITALIAN CASA DEI BAMBINI—A DAY WITH THE CHILDREN'S ACTIVITIES

What has been said thus far is almost certain to have aroused in the minds of many readers the question, "How in the world does Dr. Montessori accomplish all this?" or, perhaps the more skeptical exclamation, "It can't be done, by Dr. Montessori or anyone else!" How *can* children teach themselves? How can they learn without detailed verbal instructions from a teacher?

How does a boy learn to climb an apple tree? By being turned loose in company with the tree at that period of his life when he feels a surging natural impulse to climb trees. A boy of three can play about the foot of an apple tree day after day and no more think of climbing it than we of walking the ridge pole of our house. A man of twenty-one can play tennis, or plough, under the tree's branches with a similar lack of monkey-like desire to climb from branch to branch. But somewhere between those ages, there is a period in every normal life when, if the opportunity is present, a vast amount of muscular agility, strength and accuracy are acquired, together with considerable physical courage, some daring, some prudence, and a fair amount of good judgment, all without the slightest need either to force or persuade the child to the acquisition of these desirable qualities.

THE PURPOSE OF THE MONTESSORI DEVICES AND THEIR EDUCATIONAL VALUE.—Now, for all intents and purposes, the Montessori apparatus, so much talked of, so scientifically and ingeniously devised, is simply composed of supplementary apple trees. It is made up of devices and inventions which are intended, *first, to stimulate the little child's natural desire to act and learn through action; second, to provide him with action which shall give him a better control of his own body and will-power; and third, which shall lead him naturally from a simple action to a more difficult one.*

TRAINS THE FIVE SENSES.—In the case of very little children this is (as far as concerns the formal Montessori apparatus sold) largely connected with the training of the senses. The importance of this detailed, direct education of the five senses may not be at first apparent. But it is evident that our five senses are our only means of conveying information to our brains about the external world which surrounds us, and it is equally evident that to act wisely and surely in the world, the brain has need of the fullest and most accurate information possible. Hence it is a foregone conclusion (once we think of it at all) that the education of all the senses of a child to rapidity, agility and exactitude, is of great importance—not at all for the sake of the information acquired at the time by the child, but for the sake of the five, finely accurate instruments which this education puts under his control.

MONTESSORI SPIRIT IS THE FIRST ESSENTIAL.—Much has been written and said about the Montessori Didactic Apparatus, but before I begin on a description of the apparatus, or of a Casa dei Bambini, I wish to make this protest. The use of her apparatus without an understanding of the underlying principles and without the spirit that animates all true Montessori work will result only in confusion and disorder. The Montessori Didactic Apparatus is a part of the system, but the most vital element is the Montessori spirit. The apparatus is immensely ingenious, it is wonderfully successful, it accomplishes its purpose with great economy of effort, but the apparatus alone is not enough. The mother on a desert island who is dominated by Dr. Montessori's love and respect for the child would accomplish much more without the formal apparatus than a mother who uses it without the sympathy and understanding requisite for success. So, dear mother, do not become discouraged if you cannot afford the apparatus. Above all have faith and confidence in your child, and your ability to put the Montessori spirit into the everyday affairs of the child's home life.

THE CASA DEI BAMBINI.—If you wish to see a typical Casa dei Bambini (which means Children's Home) you are to imagine thirty children turned loose, absolutely loose, in a big, airy room, furnished with little chairs and tables, light enough for the little ones to handle, with room outdoors, close at hand, where the children may run and play when they feel like it. You are to imagine a quiet, gentle, alert, nearly always silent superintendent, to whom all those little self-teachers turn for advice in their educational career; a piano in one corner of the room, to the music of which once in a while those children who feel like it dance and play. There are soft rugs on the floor, on which those children who feel tired may lie down and rest whenever they like. On the walls there are pleasant pictures of subjects suitable for little children. There are window-boxes of plants, tended by the little pupils; there are in one corner some little washstands with small bowls and pitchers where the children wash their own faces and hands, whenever they are dirtied by their work or play. In fact,

the room and its furnishings are exactly like what
every mother would like to give her own children
in her own home. The Casa dei Bambini is truly
a "Children's Home"—a place for self-reliant work
and contented play. Such a home centers and holds
within its walls the child's every interest, and how
completely and happily children are at home in it!

FEEL A RESPONSIBILITY.—The children learn to
feel, because they are allowed to, a real responsibility for the condition of this, their very own home.
Before they begin the morning's work, the schoolroom is cleaned by themselves, using tiny brooms
and dustpans, just the right size for their little
hands, and they make their own morning toilets
neatly and cheerfully at the little washstands. They
all seem like brothers and sisters of one big family, living the happiest and sanest of family lives
together in one big, well-furnished nursery. They
forms groups of two or three, over some difficult
problem; or four or five in a game with some part
of the apparatus which needs a number of children
together; or ten or twelve in a ring-around-the-rosy
game to the music of the piano. Out in the playground, bright with flowers and plants of their
own tending, there are always some children who
are racing about in an Italian version of "black-
man" or "blindman's buff." No one makes the
slightest effort to induce them to stop playing in

order to come and learn their letters or the simpler processes of arithmetic. They do so of their very own accord. It has been found, first, that although they are free to do so if they wish, they no more wish to spend all their time in playing children's games than workers in a candy factory desire to consume chocolate drops all the time.

VALUE OF FREE-WILL OVER ENFORCED ATTENTION.—The second discovery is of even greater importance than the first; is in fact of such vital importance that it cannot be too often stated and emphasized in any writing about this system. This is the discovery that one moment of *real* attention, given of the child's own free will, with actual vivifying interest back of it, is worth more educationally than hours of enforced listening to a teacher teach. Such a moment of real attention is worth more because it is worth everything, while the enforced listening to teaching is worth nothing.

LUNCHEON IN THE CASA DEI BAMBINI.—The children, as a rule, busy themselves happily with the different parts of the apparatus most of the morning. Towards noon, preparations for luncheon begin. The children take turns in doing this work, four or five being charged every day with the responsibility of setting the tables, bringing in the soup tureens, and serving their little mates. There is no better description of this most interesting and valuable part of the routine of the day than the passage in Dr. Montessori's own book, *The Montessori Method, page 348:* "Any one who has watched them setting the table must have passed from one surprise to another. Little four-year-old waiters take the knives and forks and spoons and distribute them to the different places; they carry trays holding as many as five water glasses, and finally they go from table to table, carrying tureens full of hot soup. Not a mistake is made, not a glass is broken, not a drop of soup is spilled. All during the meal, unobtrusive little waiters watch the table assiduously; not a child empties his soup-plate without being offered more; if he is ready for the next course, a waiter briskly carries off his soup-plate. Not a child is forced to ask for more soup, or to announce that he has finished.

"Remembering the usual condition of four-year-old children, who cry, who break whatever they touch, who need to be waited on, everyone is deeply moved by the sight I have just described, which evidently results from the development of energies deeply latent in the human soul. I have often seen spectators moved to tears at this banquet of little ones."

EXERCISE THEIR OWN CHOICE.—After lunch, the children again choose freely their own occupations. Some run out to play on the playground; some water the plants under their especial care; some take naps as long as they like. By far the greater number, however, return to the Montessori apparatus and occupy themselves with that fascinating material until it is time for them to go back to their parents' homes—for they consider the schoolroom as their *own* home. And well they may, for everything in it is devised scientifically, carefully, ingeniously and devotedly to the comfort, profit, enjoyment and self-education of children from three to seven. That is certainly not true of the average home in Italy or America, but if it were, how much more interesting to the child and more helpful would be the environments of the home!

IV

USE OF THE APPARATUS WITH COMPRE-
HENSIVE AND PRACTICAL DIRECTIONS
TO THE MOTHER OR TEACHER

We in America who have children between the ages of two and seven can not as yet send our children to a Casa dei Bambini. Therefore, if we wish our children to profit by the great work of Dr. Montessori, we must do the next best thing, and give them the Montessori training in our own homes. The fact that we have only the children of our own home to deal with, as compared to the thirty in the Casa dei Bambini should not lessen the sense of responsibility or the diligence with which we strive to make daily application of the Montessori principles. The mother has some advantages which the superintendent of the Montessori schoolroom does not have. She has the children constantly with her, and she can, if she will, turn into a Montessori exercise almost everything the child does in the course of his waking hours. These valuable and constantly present opportunities for supplementary Montessori work in ordinary home

COLOR SPOOLS

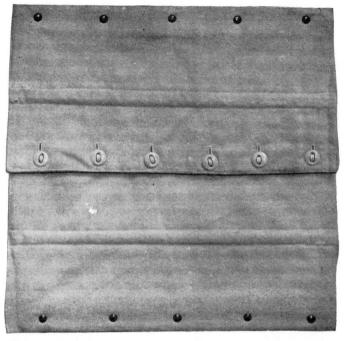

Buttoning and Lacing Frames
(To be used in Exercise Two)

II.

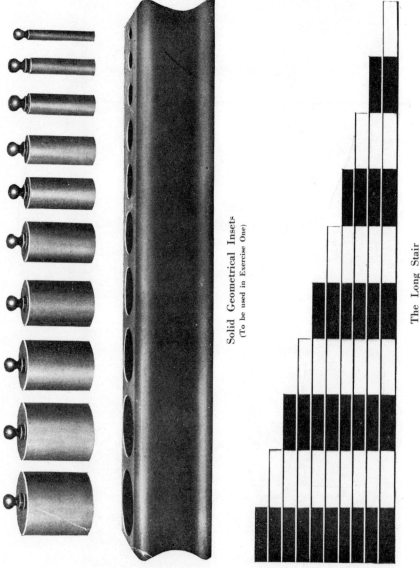

Solid Geometrical Insets
(To be used in Exercise One)

The Long Stair
(To be used in Exercise Six)

The Tower
(To be used in Exercise Four)

Broad Stair
(To be used in Exercise Five)

IV.

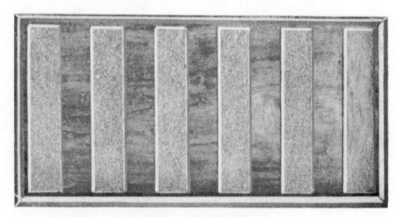

Sandpaper Boards
(To be used in Exercises Seven and Eight)

V.

Color Boxes
(To be used in Exercises Sixteen and Seventeen)

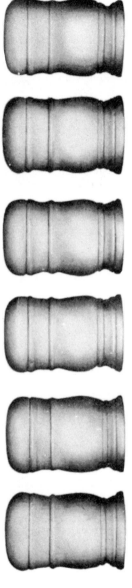

Sound Boxes
(To be used in Exercise Ten)

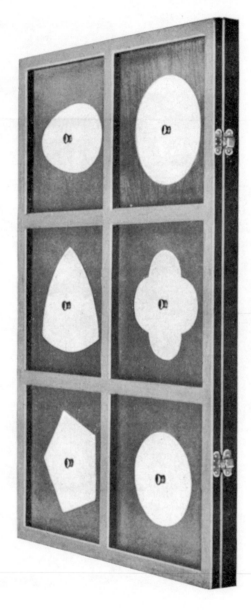

Plane Geometric Insets
(To be used in Exercises Eleven and Twelve)

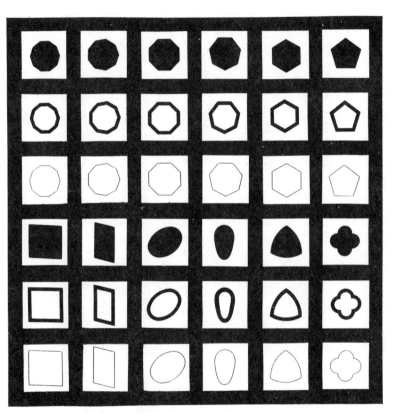

Plane Geometric Forms
(To be used in Exercise Thirteen)

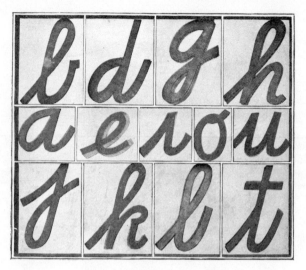

Part of Movable Alphabet
(To be used in Exercise Nineteen)

Computing Boxes
(To be used in Exercises Twenty-three and Twenty-four)

life will be touched upon as the regular apparatus is described and explained in the following lessons. But this treatment must be considered only suggestive. Every mother with any of the usual American adaptability and ingenuity can and will be able, after reading these hints, to devise a hundred new exercises for her children—exercises which will develop the typically Montessori qualities of *muscular accuracy, bodily poise, mental ability, and moral responsibility.*

Let us suppose that the box containing the Montessori apparatus comes into the home when the three-year-old child for whom it is intended is asleep. The mother takes her time to look over the large collection of queer-looking objects and, if she is wise, puts away, for the present, everything but the simplest of the Buttoning Frames and the three sets of Solid Geometric Insets.

EXERCISE ONE

TO FIX THE CHILD'S ATTENTION ON SIZE AND FORM

SOLID GEOMETRICAL INSETS.—These comprise three series of wooden cylinders set in corresponding holes in a thick, smoothly planed board. There are ten cylinders to each of the three series. In the first, the height of the cylinders is constant and the diameter varies; in the second series, the diameter is constant and the height varies; in the third series, the cylindrical form alone is constant, height and diameter varying. With these insets, the child, working independently, learns to discriminate objects according to thickness, height and size, and the material used controls the error.

When the child wakes up, he is told there are some new playthings in the house, and one of the Solid Geometric Series is shown him. As a rule, he needs no further supervision in the use of this piece of apparatus, since it is self-corrective. If he gets a small cylinder in the big hole, when he comes to the small hole, the big cylinder will not go in it, and he is forced to look back to correct his own mistake. Here, as in the use of all the Montessori apparatus, it is well to remember that the best thing one can do for the child is to let him alone as much as possible. "Hands off!" is the motto for adults in adopting the Montessori system for a child. The important thing is not that the cylinders shall all be put back in the right holes, but that the child *shall do it himself!* Any ordinarily active, right-minded baby of three will fight for this right himself, pushing away help and crying *"Let me,"* and the adults should religiously respect this desire to begin a life of self-independence. And yet, of course, adult brains can often devise some method of using the apparatus which will make the process of learning self-independence easier for the child. One of the discoveries made by Dr. Montessori is that the sense of touch is very much more developed in little children than the sense of sight; that is, that they can tell more about an object after they have handled it than if they have merely looked at it. So that in the case of the solid geometric insets, it is well to explain to a child who has difficulty in getting the cylinders back in the right hole that if he holds a cylinder by the little knob with the fingers of his left hand and passes the forefinger of his right hand around the base of it, and then around the opening into which he thinks it ought to fit, that he will probably be more accurate than if he merely looks at the two objects.

It is well that the mother should understand just why the child should be interested in these exercises. There are two fundamental traits of childhood involved: first, any normal child takes a great interest in putting objects in rows; second, any child is delighted when he can put an object into an opening. Combining these two traits of childhood, we have a fascinating educational device. The child is not only happily employed but he is learning something that is of value. He is learning to discriminate between different objects. Although he does it unconsciously, he is forming an idea of spacial relations. He is developing concentration because this play, fascinating as it is, requires concentration. When he discriminates between the different cylinders, he must necessarily form primitive judgments. This brief description will, I hope, give you some idea of the educational value of these first simple exercises.

When the child can successfully put the various cylinders in their respective openings, the exercises can be made more complex by giving all the cylinders to the child and only one of the bases. This requires a greater discrimination, making the exercise more complex. The cylinders can also be used a little later in teaching nomenclature, to show the difference between thick and thin, thicker and thinner, high and low, higher and lower, etc.

After he has mastered the simpler exercises, the child may be blindfolded or, looking in another direction, place the various cylinders into the openings. These exercises bring into play the tactile and muscular senses, both of which are very acute in small children. Since the child delights to feel of objects, it will not be long until he will take a great interest in the game of "seeing with his fingers." These sets of cylinders are perhaps the simplest of all the equipment and at the same time I might say they have proved the most fascinating for small children.

THE TRACING OF FORMS, "THE BEGINNINGS" OF

WRITING.—The child should be cautioned (and his mother should take pains about this in all Montessori exercises) to make the motions always from the left to the right, in the directions in which the writing is done, for these exercises, unlikely as it seems, are the beginnings of writing and reading. Then he should be left to "play" with this new toy, as long as his interest lasts, which will vary greatly according to the degree of development reached, the temperament of the child, and even his state of health. When he is perfectly well and rested and not hungry, he can do much better work than otherwise—very much like the rest of us! His attention to the exercise must, of course, be spontaneous, brought about by the interest of the task given, and if the task does not happen to interest that particular child at that particular moment, nothing can be gained by forcing him or even coaxing him to go on with it. He will return to it another day, or perhaps even an hour later, of his own accord.

EXERCISE TWO

FOR CO-ORDINATING MOVEMENTS OF THE FINGERS

THE BUTTONING OR DRESSING FRAMES.—There are eight of the dressing or buttoning frames. Any one or more of these can be used effectively without association with the others. On six wooden frames are mounted six pieces of cloth of varying textures, to be joined by means of large buttons and buttonholes, automatic fasteners, small buttons and buttonholes, hooks and eyes, colored ribbons for bow-tying, and lacing through eyelets. The remaining two frames are mounted with leather pieces, one of which simulates shoe lacing and the other shoe buttoning, the latter involving the use of the button hook. These exercises are for the development of co-ordinate movements of the fingers. The child is taught to dress himself without his really knowing that a lesson is being taught him, and when the frames are mastered, his first desire is to make a practical application of his new ability.

The Buttoning Frame, or the frame with "hooks and eyes," should be brought out first, and the method of fastening and unfastening explained in the usual Montessori way; that is, as briefly as possible. It is often best not to say anything, but merely to go through the exercises one's self, unbuttoning or unhooking the cloth, buttoning or hooking it up again, and handing the frame to the child. In most cases he at once sets to work, and even though his first efforts seem to the observing mother incredibly clumsy and slow, she must keep her hands off, and let him work out his own problems. The only rule should be that if he does not wish to play with the apparatus, or when he grows tired of its use, he should put it away; and for that purpose it is very essential that there should be a well defined place, which the child can easily reach, for every one of his belongings—not only for the Montessori apparatus, but for his other toys and for his clothing. The hooks should be low, so that little arms can reach them, and the drawers where clothing is put away should be easy to open and shut. Three years is none too young to begin the habit of order, which, like so many other good habits, may be acquired painlessly at an early age, although so nearly impossible to inculcate after the bad habits have become fixed. The exercises with the dressing frames are not necessarily for the developing of the different senses. The primary object is to develop the muscular co-ordination to strengthen the child's little fingers. These materials carry out Dr. Montessori's ideas of simplicity, self-correction and general attractiveness. They are so simple that the child at once understands the meaning of the game, and in working with these various materials his little fingers and hands are so strengthened that he may successfully take up more complex and difficult work. Of course, one of the incidents of this work is that he learns to dress and undress himself. This, it should be remembered, is not the primary factor that Dr. Montessori has in mind. It is incidental to the general muscular co-ordination that is effected.

EXERCISE THREE

SUPPLEMENTARY EXERCISES TEACHING THE PRACTICAL
APPLICATION OF KNOWLEDGE GAINED WITH
THE APPARATUS

One obvious result sought in all these exercises
is the beginning in the child's mind of the habit
of concentration to the task in hand. The insets
are primarily intended, as already stated, to teach
the child to distinguish between differences in dimension and form, and this can be taught by supplementary exercises in almost any room of the house.

First.—In the dining-room he can be given a
pile of spoons of differing size, teaspoons, table-
spoons, soup-spoons, coffee-spoons, etc., and the
suggestion made to him that it would be fun to
separate them into piles according to their sizes.
In most cases, this impromptu Montessori exercise
can be depended upon to amuse the child for an
astonishingly long period, and it is, of course, excellent training for his capacity to distinguish accurately between objects similar but of differing size.
In the kitchen, a pile of pans and covers will afford
a great deal of valuable practice in distinguishing
which cover will fit which pan.

Second.—Out of doors, a pile of stones of differing sizes can be divided into several piles of the
same size. Most mothers will be surprised at the

Exercising the sense of touch combined with muscular
sense in learning the form of letters

Working with the Montessori Movable Alphabet

vast and inextinguishable interest taken in such simple exercises by the average healthy child of three or over. The gain in accuracy of eye and brain is too obvious to need discussion.

Third.—The buttoning frames are intended first of all to teach the child to use his hands and fingers accurately and well, and next to enable him to dress himself as far as may be. This is very important, for the first thing to be done for a little child is to release him as quickly as possible from the prison of babyishness—to make it possible for him to take care of himself, and not to depend upon the services of others. As his clothes are nearly always fastened with buttons, it is essential that considerable time be devoted to teaching him how to manage these, or, rather, that he shall be allowed to take the time necessary to learn this. For he has a natural fund of desire to manage himself which makes him eager to learn. The buttoning frames, being of cloth tightly stretched on wood, are easier for him to manage than the buttons on his own clothes, although as soon as he begins to try to button his own coats and waists, he should be allowed all the time he needs for his first clumsy and ineffectual attempts. Remember, he should be allowed all the time he needs—not all the help he needs! For if he is often helped, he will fall into the vicious, invalid's habit of waiting for other people to serve him. Care should be taken that the buttons on his clothes are large and easily grasped by his little wandering fingers, and that, if possible, they should be put on in positions where he can get at them without too much wriggling and twisting. This is more important by far than that they should be handsome, or set on according to the latest fashion.

Fourth.—In addition to the buttons and hooks on his own clothes, it is a good idea to give him other things which fasten in that way; and a large doll which can wear his own clothes is a very good aid at this stage of his development. The doll is most easily made and most serviceable, constructed of cloth and stuffed. As it can wear the clothes of the child, he has a large wardrobe ready at hand to play with, and he can manage it much better than the usual doll's clothes with minute buttons and buttonholes, which are hard even for adult fingers. It is well to remember, here and always, that, as a rule, children must have large objects to deal with, rather than small, if their eyesight is to be preserved without injury.

Fifth.—The lace and ribbon frames are more difficult to use and are, of course, to be held back until the child is older, perhaps four or five. From time to time, they should be brought out and a simple experiment made of the child's capacity to deal with it. If he does not at once show interest in the problem of bow-knots and laces, and more of a capacity to struggle with the construction of them than on the last trial, the frame should be taken away, without comment, and not tried again until more progress has been made in the other exercises. It must be remembered, as a general rule for the use of the Montessori exercises, and in general in the training of little children, that no prolonged attempt should ever be made to coax them to continue an exercise which does not interest them. If they show no spontaneous interest, they are not ready for it, and time is only wasted by any attempt to force their inclination. When they are ready, they can learn in ten minutes what three hours of dreary enforced practice was not able to teach them.

EXERCISE FOUR

EXERCISES FOUR, FIVE AND SIX ARE ALSO FOR THE FURTHER CULTIVATION OF THE CHILD'S VISUAL PERCEPTION OF DIFFERENCE IN DIMENSION AND FORM

THE BLOCK TOWER.—After the child has had a day or so of practice with the Geometric Insets and Buttoning Frames, allowing him to take them up and lay them down at will, it is time to bring out the blocks composing the Tower. The Tower is a series of ten wooden cubes, decreasing in size. Almost every nursery possesses such blocks, but few mothers are aware of their educational value or of the distinctive use to which blocks of graduated size should be put. Their use should not be confused with that of the ordinary "building blocks,"—cube blocks of unvarying size. With the Tower blocks there are definite problems of classification and discrimination to be solved, and to get the benefit of them, the child must use them in the one correct way.

The mother builds up the Tower before the child's eyes, placing the largest block first, then the next smaller one, and so on down to the tiny little cube at the top. Then she knocks it all down, and if her child is the average child, he needs no more incentive to duplicate the performance and to begin to educate himself as to graduations of size. When he begins to construct the Tower himself, the difficult thing for the mother to do is to avoid giving him elaborate instructions: "No, no, Jimmy—not that one—that's not the next size—don't you see the one by your hand is bigger?" etc., etc., etc. The only good Jimmy can get of this exercise is by learning to see for himself which is the bigger block, and to do this his mother must let him alone. She need not be surprised if he makes one odd mistake continually, even after he has learned quite deftly to construct the Tower. A great many children find it difficult to begin the Tower with the biggest block. They begin it with the next biggest, and, when they have finished, find that they cannot place the largest one without tearing down the whole structure. The psychological processes involved in this mistake are too complicated to explain here. I mention it, lest some anxious mother should think her own three-year-old especially deficient in the capacity to distinguish between sizes.

One exercise that can be profitably carried out is to give the Tower to the child and have him carry it, let us say, from one part of the room to another. In all probability, his first attempt will be far from successful. Let him take his own time in the rebuilding of it, and then make another attempt. Finally, he will be able to carry it very successfully from one part of the room to another, thus showing the self-control that is developed. Many mothers have also found that the child is interested in the blindfold exercises with the Tower. This exercise merely affords another means of developing the different senses.

EXERCISE FIVE

BROAD STAIR.—After the Tower, the next exercise is the Broad Stair. It is a set of ten rectangular wooden blocks, decreasing in height and width, length only being constant. This is another of the visual perception exercises. Here it may be well to mention that when a new exercise is given a child, the older ones are by no means taken away. They are left in the nursery, where he can get at them himself whenever he wishes to, and the new ones simply added to the store of his riches. Often, when the more elaborate exercises are quite mastered, a child will take pleasure in returning for a time to the simpler old friends with which he began. He should be allowed to do this quite as he wishes, his own instinct being a sure and accurate guide to what is best for him in this respect. He is doing what we all like to do occasionally—he is "reviewing" what he has learned, and making sure of his grasp on something which he has not thought of for some time.

The Broad Stair is brought out in the same quiet manner with which the child has been introduced to his other Montessori "playthings." The mother arranges the blocks in regular order starting either with the biggest or the smallest, and laying the others side by side until a regular stair is constructed. Then she mixes the blocks up, and goes away. The child, if he is ready for this exercise, at once takes it up, and in struggling to repeat his mother's feat, constructs the stair, intellectually as well as physically, and learns a new variety of dimension. Since all these blocks are the same length, and only differ in height and thickness, his problem is one degree more difficult than in the construction of the Tower.

It should be remembered about these blocks, as about all Montessori apparatus, that they should be used for the purpose for which they are intended and for no other. The child should always have, in addition, an ordinary set of plain building blocks, with which he can play in any way he pleases, and if he begins to "make houses," etc., with his Montessori blocks, his little mind, incapable of more than one idea at a time, should be redirected to the regular exercise involving the dimensions of these blocks.

EXERCISE SIX

THE LONG STAIR.—After the Tower and the Stair comes the third set of blocks, or rods, called the Long Stair. This is the most important of the three sets, as it is the foundation for instruction in arithmetic. With this set of short rectangular rods, the child learns, as he grows older, a number of the simpler processes of numeration. At first they are presented to the child just as a series of rods differing in length, the smallest one being one-tenth of the length of the longest one. The mother builds up the series, having the child notice that all the rods are red on one end, and that the stairs have a regular number of red and blue spaces from one to ten, or from the bottom to the top of the stairs. Then the series is knocked over, the rods mixed up, and the child left to put it together again himself. Children who cannot definitely count can often manage this series, and it is the greatest pleasure for the child who has just learned to count to be able to verify his numbers in this concrete way. For the present, this is all that is done with the Long Stair, but as the child progresses and develops, it will be found one of the most valuable parts of the apparatus, because the rods can be combined in many different ways, and illustrate in the plainest and most unmistakable manner many of the simpler processes of mathematics—addition, subtraction, etc. But this all comes later, and after the child has mastered other of the apparatus. Perhaps the mother will ask why Dr. Montessori uses ten blocks for each series, or, in short, what is the reason for these series. The child learns by comparisons, contrasts and classifications, just as the adult does. It is much easier for him to comprehend the different dimensions when he has the means of comparing blocks with others which vary in size. In short, the child understands the relation between the different blocks when presented in this manner.

ORDER OF EXERCISES TO BE MODIFIED ACCORDING TO CIRCUMSTANCES.—It is not desirable that we give directions for the exact use and the order of succession of the remainder of the apparatus. Children differ so widely that the mother will be forced to depend somewhat on her own judgment and intimate knowledge of the child. She will have grasped by this time the purpose of the exercises with the Montessori apparatus, which is *to give the child the fullest possible control over his own body and will-power*. The order of exercises as hereafter indicated is to be followed with any ordinary child, but this must be modified according to circumstances.

EXERCISE SEVEN

DEVELOPING THE SENSE OF TOUCH

SANDPAPER BOARD NUMBER ONE.—As a rule, the next piece of apparatus to be taken up is the Sandpaper Board, a small board, one-half of which is smooth and the other half covered with sandpaper. This fixes the child's attention on the difference between surfaces. Sometimes this is one of the very first apparatus to be used, as a distinction between rough and smooth is apt to be one which arouses the interest of a very little child. His mother takes the board in her lap, or lays it on the child's small table, and draws the little finger-tips over the smoothly planed board, saying at the same time, "smooth, smooth." Then she draws the finger-tips (always from left to right) over the rough sand-paper, saying, "rough, rough." The child very soon associates the sound with the sensation, to which his finger-tips are more alive than are deadened adult fingers, and says himself, as he touches the two surfaces, "smooth, smooth—rough, rough." After this distinction has been thoroughly learned (it may take only one lesson, or it may take two or three days), it is a good plan to try to see if he can make the distinction accurately when he is not looking at the board, purely by the sense of touch. The Italian children are always blindfolded for this exercise, and seem to enjoy it, but the American children with whom I have had experience have preferred merely to look away, up at the ceiling. The finger-tips should then be passed, always with the utmost delicacy and with the lightest possible touch, over the two surfaces, and the child asked to give the right name to what he is touching. At the first sign of mental fatigue or confusion, this exercise should be discontinued, although it may be taken up again after a half-hour's rest and change of occupation. The child's fingers should always be trained from left to right. If the child from the very beginning is directed to trace from left to right, he has effected the first simple muscular co-ordination that he will use a little later in writing, as we always write from left to right. In all probability, the child will enjoy touching the smooth surface very much, and it is interesting to note the change of expression on his face as he changes from the smooth to the rough.

EXERCISE EIGHT

SANDPAPER BOARD NUMBER TWO.—When this simpler of the sandpaper boards has been mastered, the child may go to the next form, in which the sandpaper is arranged in alternate strips on the smoothly planed board. This is, of course, more complicated, and the blindfolded child may soon "lose his head" and not be able to distinguish accurately between the sensations. He should be encouraged to take plenty of time, and to allow his fingertips to play freely across the surface. When he can tell quickly, accurately, and without mental fatigue, whether he is touching a rough or smooth strip, the beginning of the child's education of his tactile sense is well made. He has taken the first step, which counts so much, and will go on steadily to more complicated conquests. In this exercise, the child is also learning to follow a raised surface with his little fingers. This is of great value to him as a preliminary to the sandpaper letters. After he has mastered this simple exercise, he has one of the first requisites necessary for successful work with the sandpaper letters.

EXERCISE NINE

FOR THE FURTHER DEVELOPMENT OF THE CHILD'S TACTILE SENSE

In the formal Montessori apparatus, the small cabinet containing seven drawers is filled with various fabrics. These fabrics consist of two pieces of the following materials: velvet, silk, wool, fine and coarse linen, and fine and coarse cotton. It is very important that absolutely pure fabrics should be used for these first exercises; in short, the mother should be quite sure that the linen she is using is not partly cotton. Of course, if the regular Montessori apparatus is used, all of these precautions are provided for. These can be supplemented by any ragbag, and from the infinitely diversified fabrics used in the furnishing of any home. When this "playing" with fabrics is first begun, the child is allowed to handle the different pieces of cloth, and his attention is called to the difference in their texture. He is told their names, one or two at a time, the mother taking the greatest pains to pronounce the words clearly, distinctly, and SLOWLY. When he has learned to distinguish them by looking at them, the next step, as with the sandpaper boards, is to distinguish them by the sense of touch only. The child can be blindfolded, or can look up at the ceiling, and, sitting in front of a mixed-up pile of the pieces, takes them up one at a time, pronouncing their names. When he has done this enough times so that he is quite sure of himself (usually after a week of playing with the pieces at intervals), he can go on to some of the fascinating "games" to be played with them. If there are other children in the family, the playing of "games" is easier, but even for an only child they are possible.

SUPPLEMENTARY EXERCISES AND GAMES INVOLVING THE SENSE OF TOUCH.—*First.*—The pieces are divided into two piles, each having the same number of pieces of the same fabrics. Then the mother picks out a piece of velvet, without naming it, asks the child if he can find a piece like it in his pile (of course, without looking). This is always productive of much excited fumbling in the pieces, and much delicate fingering of them by sensitive little finger-tips, and finally much triumph when the matching bit of velvet is discovered. It may be said in passing that it is usually well to begin with either velvet or silk, as those fabrics are so markedly different from others that the problem is easier for a beginner. If two children play this "game," the victor is the one who first finds the piece of velvet without looking at his pile.

Second.—The mother's ingenuity can devise many other variations on this game, and can see to it that the child goes on observing the fabrics used in different parts of the house, the materials of which his own dresses are made, the stuff used in upholstery, table linen, curtains, etc. He can also be told the names of the different materials used in building a house—wood, iron, tin, glass, stone, and brick; and the materials of cooking utensils—china, tin, copper, etc. There is an infinite variety of material in the humblest home which can be the most valuable educational apparatus for the well-trained child, even in quite early childhood. Once the child's interest in this problem is aroused, he will in most cases go on educating himself, and all the parent needs to do is to have the patience necessary to answer innumerable questions.

Third.—Games with Balls, Squares, Triangles, etc.—Another "game" for developing the sense of touch with materials other than fabrics is played in the Casa dei Bambini with solid wooden geometric forms of differing shapes—balls, squares, triangles, etc. The child is blindfolded, and pulls these things, one at a time, out of a bag, identifying them solely by fingering them over. In the home this can be "played" with any material at hand with which the child is familiar. He can be blindfolded and try to identify objects in a miscellaneous heap on the table before him, consisting of toy animals, spoons, forks, brushes, combs, dolls, trays—anything in the room which will not hurt him, and is not breakable. Very little children always experience the greatest joy in thus proving that they can see "with their fingers," and learn to receive extremely accurate impressions through their sensitive and cultivated little finger-tips.

EXERCISE TEN

TRAINING THE SENSE OF HEARING

SOUND BOXES.—But the sense of touch is not the only one of the child's five senses which can be improved by direct training. The sense of hearing is greatly developed and made more serviceable for after years, if given reasonable practice. The Montessori apparatus provides the wooden Sound Boxes, filled with different substances—sand, gravel, flaxseed, stones, etc., which give out sounds differing in quality and loudness, when shaken. The child's attention can be thus fixed, for the first time, on a definite attempt to distinguish between loud and low noises, as he shakes these little boxes close to his ear, and attempts to arrange them in order according to their degree of noise.

In all probability, the child has heard noises of this character, but he has not had an opportunity to compare or to contrast such noises. This exercise affords an opportunity for such discrimination. As a rule, the children take a great deal of interest in this simple exercise and they show a marked difference in their ability to discriminate between the various substances.

SUPPLEMENTARY EXERCISES AND "GAMES."--But this simple exercise needs to be supplemented by other "games" which fix the attention on sounds. These can be devised most easily with "hide-and-seek" games. The mother hides and blows very softly a little horn, by means of which the child traces her; or she calls the child's name in the lowest possible whispers, as he, blindfolded, tries to locate her in the room by his hearing. Any of the common children's games, "blindman's buff," "still-pond-no-more-moving," etc., played with a blindfold, are excellent exercises for the same purpose of sharpening the hearing and training the child to receive accurate impressions through his ears.

Out of doors, long-distance calling may be used for this purpose, to accustom the child to determine the direction from which any noise comes.

As to musical sounds, most children who are young enough for this Montessori training are too young to distinguish pitch at all accurately. Of music they receive practically nothing but rhythm, although they are fond of marching to a tune which has strongly marked time, and this is a good exercise for them, in its place.

A spontaneous writing lesson. These children have reached the point where, as Montessori says, they "explode into writing."

Montessori Long Stair Game

EXERCISE ELEVEN

PREPARATORY EXERCISE FOR TEACHING THE CHILD TO WRITE

PLANE GEOMETRIC INSETS.—Very soon after the child's first introduction to the Montessori apparatus, he can begin his use of the Plane Geometric Insets. These sets consist of a six-drawer cabinet, thirty-six geometrical insets, and a pattern in an adjustable frame, making possible any desired combination of forms. The insets are made of pieces of smooth wood, painted blue, cut in different shapes, and with a little knob-like handle in the center. These insets fit into holes or openings cut in a rectangular natural colored piece of wood. The first of the series of six drawers contains insets of strongly contrasted forms; the second drawer contains a series of six Polygons; the third drawer, a series of six Circles, diminishing in size; the fourth drawer, a series of Quadrilaterals containing one square and five rectangles; the fifth drawer, a series of six Triangles, and the sixth drawer contains Oval, Ellipse, Flower Forms, etc. These are so important and have such a vital part to play in the training of the child to write, that the mother should be especially careful in the way they are used. The entire thirty-six different shapes should not, of course, be put before the child at the beginning but only a drawer of the most strongly contrasted shapes—triangles, oblong, etc. He should be taught at the very start (as in the case of the solid geometric insets) to aid his sight by touch. While he holds the inset by the little knob with his left hand, he traces the outline of the inset with his right forefinger, and from left to right, or in the direction in which writing is done. Then, while still holding the inset, he traces around the outline of the depression into which he thinks the inset he holds would fit. In finding the right opening, he is guided more by his finger-tips than by his eyes. It is quite important to establish this habit of tracing the outline with his fingers, as it has a vital bearing on learning to write.

As the child masters the tray of the more simple forms so that he finds it easy for him to place the insets in the corresponding opening, the less simple forms should be given him, a few at a time. After learning to distinguish between a triangle and a circle quickly and accurately, the next day he should be given two triangles and two circles of different sizes, to sharpen his sense of shape and dimension. After a time, usually a fortnight or so, he should be able to replace in the correct openings six triangles of differing shapes, and six circles of differing sizes. When he has learned to do that, he has attained a mastery of his little brain and a capacity to make it work accurately, of which his mother may well be proud.

It is perhaps well to give here the warning which can never be too often sounded—not to force the child's attention to this, any more than to any other problem. He is the best judge of when mental fatigue sets in, and at the least sign of inattention, the tray of insets should be put away and some romping game outdoors played, or a quiet story told. The mother is so apt to become fascinated with the rapid advance of the child's mentality that she can hardly forbear urging him a trifle to go a step or so beyond his natural inclination.

EXERCISE TWELVE

REPLACING THE INSETS BLINDFOLDED

When the insets have become old friends, it is well to try blindfolding the child, and setting him the new problem of replacing the geometric forms by the sense of touch only. Here it is well to go back again to first principles and to begin once more with the easiest forms, until he grows accustomed to depending on his touch only. This is splendid practice, and a child who has had it grows astonishingly keen in his capacity to take in accurate impressions from his finger-tips. How valuable the ability to work without looking at what is being done, can be estimated from the experience of almost any variety of hand-worker. The old grandmother who knits without once looking at her needle can work all day long without a particle of fatigue, while the knitter who needs to be verifying each stitch by her eyes soon tires them out and must either stop working or suffer a violent headache. The stenographer who writes by touch has a tremendous advantage over the other who needs to use her eyes. A large part of our modern eye-strain and nervous headaches, and even nervous prostration, comes, so the doctors say, from the constant use of the eyes in processes which might be cared for by the other senses, if they were only well trained. So that the Montessori child, learning to distinguish between his insets without looking at them, is learning a mental habit which will be of incalculable benefit to him throughout life.

Dr. Montessori lays great stress upon the value of the work with these wooden geometric insets. They are so practical and at the same time so fascinating that the child learns a great deal in working with them. The primary object is that the child should learn form; that is, that he should see the difference between various objects. Ordinarily, this is a very tedious task for the child, but Dr. Montessori, by means of her self-correcting apparatus, has made a game that appeals to normal

children. The mother should not be at all surprised
if after a few weeks of play with this apparatus
the child should begin to point out various objects
in his environment, comparing them with certain
insets he has learned to know. These exercises
are very important. The mother should take the
care and the time that may be necessary for the
child to reap the greatest benefits from the work.

EXERCISE THIRTEEN

WITH WHICH THE CHILD'S COMPREHENSION PASSES
FROM SOLID OBJECTS TO THE PLANE LINE, FROM
THE CONCRETE TO THE ABSTRACT

PLANE GEOMETRIC FIGURES REPRODUCED IN THREE
SERIES OF CARDS.—After the final mastery of the
geometric insets, the child is given a series of cards,
representing the same forms as those of his insets.
In the first of these three series, the forms are cut
out of solid blue paper and mounted on white cards;
in the second, the forms are cut out of heavy line
drawings and mounted on the cards, and in the
third, the outline or form is represented only by
a thin blue line, such as is drawn by any pencil.

The child mixes up, say, six or eight of these
cards, and six or eight corresponding insets, and
then sets himself the task of putting the insets on
the corresponding card. Here he has not the sense

of touch to guide him, and learns gradually the meaning of the line, passing from the solid blue form to the form merely drawn in outline.

After the child has played with these various cards for some time he will have acquired a very definite idea of symbolism. That is, it will be comparatively easy for him to understand how a series of lines can stand for an object. Ordinarily, it is not difficult for the child to see the connection between a photograph and an object, but with an abstract line it is entirely different. What is there in the symbols c-a-t that would connect them with a cat? Dr. Montessori believes that the child should understand symbolism before the alphabet is taken up. When the child has mastered all of the various exercises with these geometric cards, and thus gained a definite understanding of symbolism, it will be comparatively easy for him to get the relation between a written word and the object which that word represents. Dr. Montessori at all times goes from the simple to the complex, from the concrete to the abstract. With this simple explanation I trust the mother will understand the significance of these exercises.

EXERCISE FOURTEEN

INVOLVING THE FIRST USE OF THE PENCIL

PLANE GEOMETRICAL INSETS MADE IN METAL.—
And with this recognition of the line, might go
very well with the average child the beginning of
the use of the pencil. This exercise is done with
the Plane Geometric Insets made of metal.
Accompanying the metal insets in the formal
Montessori apparatus are two wooden trays with
sloping tops, large enough to hold three of the
metal insets and intended to be placed by the
child on his own table. It is, of course, unnecessary to point out that a small table and chair,
just the right size for a child, are essentials in
Montessori or any other right training for childhood. The child puts a piece of white paper on
the wooden tray or on his own table, then places
the square inset over the paper and lifts out the
central piece by its little knob. The white paper
shows through the hole (see x in illustration) in
the shape of the inset. The child is given a
pencil and is shown, once, very briefly and simply,
how to hold it and how to trace around the outline of the inset. He is apt to make bad work
of this at first, as this is the very first use of
the pencil, but his interest almost certainly carries
him through the first difficulties. To begin with

he simply traces the outline, lifts off the metal inset and admires the design on the paper beneath. The metal edge of the inset is a guide to his staggering little pencil and before long he will be able to make a good, clear outline, joining the ends neatly.

EXERCISE FIFTEEN

THE USE OF COLORED CRAYONS

FIRST LESSON IN DRAWING.—When this has been accomplished the child is furnished with a box of colored crayons, and invited to fill in the "picture" he has made with strokes of his crayon. The fact that he is working in color stimulates his interest, and few children need more spur to advance than the simple permission to use the crayons. At first, and for many days, his efforts to fill in the outlines will be ludicrous in their inaccuracy. He should not be corrected, and should be allowed to pass from one form to another as often as he pleases, being supplied with an unlimited amount of paper and leisure for this new undertaking. Little by little, as he works at this accomplishment, along with other Montessori "games" he begins to "get the hang of it," in our vernacular phrase. The lines become more and more parallel, fewer and fewer go wildly outside the line enclosing the outline, and finally the geometric form is shown in color on the white paper almost as though it had been printed. This advance is not rapid, however, in the case of most children, and nothing should be done to hurry it. Occasionally a child gets tired of the whole process and will play with other things for several days without recurring to his "drawing," although on the other hand, some children are, from the first, so fascinated by the problem that they can hardly let it alone. These exercises afford the first direct preparation for writing and design. From the very beginning the child acquires a free, easy muscular movement. After these exercises the work of free designing with crayons and water colors may be successfully taken up.

Meal-times and Nap-times Not to Be Interfered With.—The child should be allowed to choose his own time for working at this (provided, of course, that it does not interfere with some necessary regulations of the household, meal-times or nap-times) and to spend as much or as little time over it as he wishes, although if there seems any likelihood that he has really forgotten it, his attention may be called to it again.

EXERCISE SIXTEEN

TRAINING THE EYE; THE MATCHING OF COLORS

COLOR BOXES AND COLOR "GAMES."—At about the same stage of development that the geometric insets are first given to a child, the color boxes can be shown him and the color "games" begun. The color boxes are sets of spools, wound with silk of varying shades, eight of the main colors, and eight shades of each. At first the child is shown only two strongly contrasting colors, red and blue, for instance. The name is pronounced clearly and distinctly, holding up the corresponding color. When the child has grasped this the colors are allowed to lie on the table and the mother says, "Give me red," or "Give me blue." When the child has progressed this far (this may be the next day, or even two or three days after the first introduction) the teacher or mother holds up a spool and asks, "What is this?" When the child can answer correctly, "blue" or "red," he has thoroughly learned those two colors and can progress to another one. When the eight main colors have been learned in this way, the child can begin to match them. Four spools are laid on the table, two red and two blue (of course of exactly the same shade). The child picks out the two red ones and lays them side by side, and then does the same for the blue. From this he can go by degrees until there are sixteen spools on the table, eight pairs, which he must put together. This is a "game" which seldom ever fails to arouse the interest and attention of the most lethargic child. And this also soon shows the mother if there is any color-blindness present.

EXERCISE SEVENTEEN

DIFFERENTIATION OF COLORS.—After the matching has been mastered, the next step is to differentiate between light and dark shades of the same color, dark red and light pink, for instance, or dark and light blue. This goes in pairs at first also, but little by little, as the child's accuracy increases, he may go up to the eight shades of the different colors. As a rule, children acquire an appreciation and accuracy in handling colors which astonishes their ill-trained elders. Some Montessori children have become so proficient that they can "carry a color in the eye," as it is called. That is, they can look at a spool of a certain shade of purple, go across the room to a pile of spools and pick out the color matching it. This is a feat of which few elders would be capable.

GAMES AND PRACTICAL APPLICATION.—With these color spools, a variety of "games" can be

played, which any mother can invent, according
to the number and age of the children wishing
to play. They are all variations on the principle
which is used in the game of "authors," and can
be made simple or hard as circumstances direct.
Furthermore, as in the treatment of fabrics, the
child's attention is awakened to the presence of
color in everything about him, and his interest
aroused in the problem of determining the color
of the carpets, curtains, dresses, carriages, shoes,
etc., which he sees in his every-day life. In my
own family, a child of three-and-a-half came to
me the other day saying, "I've been looking
around and I can tell the color of everything in
this room, except the looking-glass, and I cannot
tell the color of that!"

The reason that Dr. Montessori uses these
little spools upon which the silk is wound is that
the child's attention is primarily directed to the
color and not to the object. The spools in themselves are very unattractive while the richly colored silk is just the opposite. Silk thread is used
because it gives a deeper, richer color, at the same
time is more practical and makes possible the
various gradations. Too much importance cannot be placed upon the developing of the chro-
matic sense in early childhood. If the child at an
early age acquires a deep interest in shades and

tints of colorings, he will not only be able to appreciate his environment much more, but this knowledge and appreciation of color will be of inestimable value to him in later years. The ethical element in such training is also very important. If the child is taught to see the beautiful and to appreciate it even in his early years it must have a marked effect upon his later life. Psychologists tell us that we are the creatures of habit and it is only reasonable to believe that if these very desirable habits can be formed in early childhood they must be very beneficial when the child reaches maturity.

EXERCISE EIGHTEEN

SPECIAL PHYSICAL AND GYMNASTIC EXERCISES FOR THE YOUNG CHILD

In connection with all these exercises with the Montessori apparatus there are a number of other exercises, chiefly gymnastic, which should be constantly in use. As soon as the child can walk at all, every effort should be made to teach him further and more definitely the art of equilibrium of his body. When we walk we continually balance our weight so that we do not fall down, and the more accurately and unconsciously we do this, the better we walk. Now, bodily poise is one of the very important factors in bodily grace and even in strength, certainly in comfort. The average child does not balance his body well, instinctively. He needs training, and he is eager and anxious for it.

1. THE CHALK LINE EXERCISE.—In the Casa dei Bambini the exercise used for this need is arranged very simply by means of a long chalk line drawn on the floor. The children are invited to see how accurately they can walk along this line without stepping off. At first the little tots cannot manage this at all. Later they learn to walk very slowly along the line, and later, when they are four or five, to run as swiftly as deer along this line without swerving once from it. A child who can do that will be able, unconsciously, to walk straight across a room to a chair, without tripping or falling over the furniture.

2. WALKING THE TWO-BY-FOUR.—A modification of this exercise can be arranged out-of-doors by laying a long piece of wood (what is usually known as a "two-by-four" or a "piece of studding") down on the ground and permitting the child to try to walk along this without falling off. He is usually ready to spend a long time at this exercise, and to return to it repeatedly. The benefit derived from it is beyond calculating.

3. ROPE-BALANCING AND WALKING BACKWARD.—

If a length of rope can be hung up where the child can reach the dangling end of it he will devise for himself a variety of exercises in balancing which will greatly increase his mastery of his body. Another exercise of great value for little children, is in walking backward. At first they need to be helped, for their little brains are so unused to reversing the processes of ordinary walking that they are quite helpless, but after a comparatively short time, they learn this new trick and practice it with delight. If possible every small child should have a little swing, just the right height for him, and a tiny springboard ending over a pile of hay or anything soft, from which he may jump and learn to balance his body in the air. He should also be encouraged to jump, not from stairs or any other elevation, for that means danger to the spine, but from one rug to another, for instance. It is surprising what advances in physical strength and mastery of his muscles is made by a child who is provided with such exercises.

4. THE BABY BALL.—Most children of three are too young to have the least capacity for throwing or catching a ball, but if a ball is hung on a long string and tossed to them, the string retards the motion just enough to make it possible for their little brains to set their muscles in action,

and they will play with great joy and profit for a long time, at this variety of "babyball."

5. WATER PLAY.—One exercise, which always delights children, and improves their table-manners insensibly, is playing with water. This, too, is rather hard to manage indoors, although not impossible. The child is furnished with a basin of water, a big spoon, and receptacles of various sizes and shapes to fill; bottles, large and small; glasses, cups, salt-cellars, etc. He is almost sure to spend much time happily engaged in filling up and emptying these vessels, and learning a great deal about the nature of water contained in receptacles. A child who has "played" in this way with water, for half an hour a day, during a month or two, will spill water from his glass at table, or be untidy in the use of his spoon, just as infrequently as the ordinary adult. (He has learned the trick! And he has had a great deal of fun while he learned it). His mother will find that he takes no more pleasure in being "messy" over his meals than she does, and as soon as he is able to avoid accidents at table, will have presentable table manners.

6. ENCOURAGE CHILD'S INVENTIVENESS.—Of course the greatest freedom should be allowed for any exercise (not injurious to the child) which his invention hits upon. The action so common among

little children of throwing themselves on a chair or stool and kicking their swinging feet in the air is an excellent exercise for the muscles of the legs and should never be discouraged. To climb up and down a short length of ladder, with the rounds set at a distance appropriate for short legs, is also very beneficial, although hard to arrange for the unfortunate child who lives in a flat, without access to a bit of out-doors all his own.

7. SHOULD SHARE HOUSEHOLD WORK.—A child who is being trained in the Montessori system should also, as soon as it is at all possible, begin to share in the work of the household. If he is provided with a small broom and dustpan, there is no reason why he should not keep his room fresh and clean, and also clean up any litter of paper or dirt which he makes in the course of the day. Setting the table is a singularly good exercise for a little child, although, of course, it is enough to begin with, if he does only a small part of the whole operation. The important element should be that what he does, he does entirely himself. If he is set to put a spoon at each place, he should be left (after due explanation, as brief as possible) to wrestle with the problem and to solve it with his own unaided invention. Later he can be given all the silver to put in place, and as he learns in his Montessori exercises, *mastery over his muscles,*

can be entrusted with china and glass at four and five years of age, which an untrained child of ten or eleven would be almost sure to break.

Pains should be taken to allow even the very little child to watch, from a comfortable position, any household operation in which he shows interest. Fortunate, indeed, the child whose mother still cooks and sews and bakes and washes, and allows her children to aid in these processes. Such children receive Montessori training without any formal apparatus.

SUMMARY OF CHILD'S ATTAINMENTS IN THE MASTERY OF HIMSELF AND HIS WORLD.—But, to return to those formal and ingeniously devised "playthings" which so wonderfully and insensibly lead the little child to a mastery of his world and himself, let us suppose that the child for whom the box of apparatus came into the home, has now been "playing" with the different pieces of apparatus described in the preceding paragraphs for about three or four months, longer if he was only three when he began, a shorter time if he was older. He has learned to replace the geometric insets blindfolded by the sense of touch only, to distinguish fabrics and materials, to build the Tower, the Broad Stair and the Long Stair, to match colors, to distinguish between noises of varying intensity, to balance himself deftly, to manage a glass of water. His mother may very well consider that it is now time to begin to teach him the beginning of reading and writing, although, as a matter of fact, the beginning was taught when he first learned the distinction between rough sandpaper and smoothly planed board.

EXERCISE NINETEEN

LEARNING TO WRITE AT THE AGE OF FOUR

SANDPAPER LETTERS.—The child is told that there is a new game to play and the little pasteboard box containing the famous Montessori sandpaper letters is brought out. This alphabet is composed of letters in plain, round script, cut out of black sand, or emery, paper and pasted upon smooth white cards. Here at once the child's past practice in learning about objects through touching them, as well as looking at them, comes into play. He is shown a letter, the mother pronounces the sound of it clearly, and shows him how to trace around it with his finger in the way one would write it. He should touch it very lightly, as he has been taught to do with all his work, and should, at first, only trace the letters when some one is watching him, to make sure he does not do it backward, or upsidedown. Make sure that he knows the vocal sound of the letter or figure he is tracing. Most children of three-and-a-half or four have seen so much of writing among the adults of their acquaintance that their curiosity is deeply aroused as to the mysterious process and they are delighted with the prospect of learning something about it. They need, as a rule, no further incentive than the statement that this is the beginning of their learning how to write.

Testing the Child's Comprehension.—As soon as a few letters are learned, the teacher, or mother, should make sure of the child's grasp of them in the same way she tested his knowledge of colors. She lays down four or five on the table and asks for a certain one. "Give me 'a,' please," or "Give me 'b.'" When the child can do this quickly and surely, she next holds one up and asks him what it is. When he can identify those first letters he can be allowed to pass on to others, and as the number even in our alphabet is quite limited, it will not be long before he has mastered all the letters.

Begins to Recognize and Spell Words.—Before that time, however, if his interest in the process is lively, he can begin to recognize words, and to compose them. If he has learned "p" and "a" he can compose the familiar word "papa," and will, in most cases, do this of his own accord if his attention is called to the pronunciation of the word. If his mother says "How would you make this word?" and then pronounces it very slowly, separating the sounds distinctly, the child will analyze the word into its component parts. "It begins with 'p,' " she says, giving the phonetic sound and not the name of the letter. Of course the child reaches instinctively for the "p," and thereafter recognizes the sound of "a," puts the two together and looks on delighted at the first word of his composition.

EXERCISE TWENTY

LEARNING TO READ THE REGULAR MOVABLE ALPHABET.—At this point the child should be presented with the Regular Movable Alphabet of cut-out script letters in stiff paper.

These come in two large, flat, pasteboard boxes with partitions dividing the same into separate compartments for each letter. There are four or five duplicates of each letter, making a like number of complete alphabets and, of course, additional letters can easily be made at home, if more are needed. These letters are not pasted on cards, like the sandpaper letters, and are easily handled and arranged as the child wishes, and with these begin his composition and recognition of words. He is not troubled, as in the old system, by the difficulty of forming the letters, as all he has had to do is to take them from the compartments and make words with them, long before his little fingers have acquired the ability to handle a pencil surely and accurately.

PRACTICE WORDS.—Of course English-speaking children have a much harder time to compose words from letters than Italian children, whose language is phonetically written. The English-speaking mother who attempts to teach her own child how to write and read, will infallibly become a convert to the ideas of the Simple Spelling Board; but, since it is out of the question for the present to change the wild insanities of English spelling, we must possess our souls in patience and exercise as much ingenuity as possible in introducing our little one to the life-long burden of an illogically spelled language. It is well for this purpose to choose for the first words, the very simplest ones, like "rat," "pin," "hen," "mama," "papa," "dog," etc., words which are not only within a child's natural comprehension, but which offer no difficulties in the way of consistent spelling. When the inevitable difficulties occur, the best that can be done is to rely on the naturally quick memory of childhood, and to fall back on the helpless statement that "it's spelled that way because that is the way it's spelled."

However, there is, even in English, quite a vocabulary of sensibly spelled words, which the child can acquire as a working beginning.

EXERCISE TWENTY-ONE

REVIEW EXERCISES WITH APPARATUS ALREADY MASTERED

First.—But although he may from now on, "play" with the movable alphabet, the use of the sandpaper letters should be steadily continued, causing him to trace them, *as they are written,* several times a day, if his interest allows. It is almost certain that he will ask to do this, as touching the letters brings home their form to his little brain much more certainly than merely looking at them. Sometimes children fail to recognize a letter when they look at it, although they can identify it perfectly after their fingers have traced it. This, being one of the essential steps in writing, must not be neglected. Children in Montessori schools, even after they can write quite fluently, very frequently go through the tracing of the sandpaper letters to refresh their memories with an exact knowledge of the shape of each letter.

Second.—At the same time that these exercises are being repeated as often as the child's interest makes possible, the exercises with "drawing," that is, tracing the outline of one of the geometric insets on the paper and filling it in with colored chalk, should also be steadily continued, for this *tracing teaches the child the use of the pencil.*

Third.—THE EXPLOSION INTO WRITING.—I quote from *A Montessori Mother* a paragraph describing the final success of these three exercises, "All these processes go on, day after day, side by side, all invisibly converging towards one end. The practice with the crayons, the recognition of the sandpaper letters by eye and touch, the revelation as to the formation of words with the movable alphabet, are so many roads leading to the painless acquisition of the art of writing. They draw nearer and nearer together, and then one day, quite suddenly, the famous "Montessori explosion into writing" occurs. The teacher of experience can tell when this explosion is imminent. First, the parallel lines which the child makes to fill and color the geometric figures become singularly even and regular; second, acquaintance with the alphabet becomes so thorough that he recognizes the letters by sense of touch only; and, third, he increases in facility for composing words with the movable alphabet. The burst into spontaneous writing usually only comes after these three conditions are present. It is to be noted that for a long time after this explosion into writing, the children continue incessantly to go through the three preparatory steps, tracing

with their fingers the sandpaper letters, filling in
the geometric forms and composing with the movable
alphabet. These are for them what scales are for
the pianist, a necessary practice for "keeping the
hand in."

Fourth.—CAUTIONS TO BE OBSERVED.—There are
several cautions to be expressed about this whole
process of teaching a child to write and read by
the Montessori method. The most important one is
against hurry. Even more consistently and steadily
than with the rest of the apparatus, the child's
natural gait ought not to be in the slightest degree
hastened by urging from outside. He will go, in
any case, so very much more rapidly, easily and
surely, than children in school, that urging him is
not necessary. The temptation with a bright, quickly
adaptable child is to attempt to "make a record."
The mother remembers reading that in Montessori
schools a child of four usually learns to write after
about six weeks of preparation and that children
of five usually spend only a month in the three
exercises before they begin to write; and she is
anxious that her child shall not fall behind. She
should bear in mind two or three factors which
make her problem different from that of the Casa
dei Bambini. First, the Casa dei Bambini child
is associated with other children, some of whom
have already learned to write, before his very eyes.

He has examples and stimulus to efforts which the single American child, working alone, lacks, in the nature of things. Furthermore, the Directress of the Montessori Casa dei Bambini was specially trained for her undertaking, and has had a great deal of experience with all sorts of children; so that she is at an advantage compared to the American mother taking up the method for the first time, and working out her own and her child's problems. There is no occasion for her to be discouraged by these facts, for success is almost sure, if she perseveres and with the right spirit. The mother should always act deliberately, she should take the greatest pains to be sure that the child understands every step before he passes on to the next, and that he has thoroughly mastered one process before he is allowed to progress to another more complicated. Above all, she should refrain from forcing the child's attention in the slightest degree.

EXERCISE TWENTY-TWO

UNDIRECTED WORK; MAINTAINING THE CHILD'S NORMAL OR EVERYDAY LIFE

All the time that this work with the drawing, and filling in of geometric forms, the tracing of the sandpaper letters and the composition of words with the movable alphabet is going on, the child's usual normal life should be continued. There should be plenty of *undirected* outdoor play, where the child's natural inventiveness has scope, "hide-and-seek" games, "tag," etc., with plenty of fun in the company of other children should be encouraged. There should be much reading to him of well-selected stories and poems suited to his age; with long hours of sleep, and a certain amount of helpful service about the household work. A "Montessori child" does not by any means signify a child who devotes most of his time to exercises with the formal "boughten" apparatus.

PLANT AND ANIMAL PETS.—He should have, if it is possible to arrange this, a plant or two of his own (even at the age of three) and a pet of his own, preferably a good-natured kitten, for he is rather young as yet for a puppy. He should assume the real responsibility for these plant and animal pets, caring for them himself. Later, he should have a little plot of ground, and learn from actual experience the wonder of growth from seeds.

HOW THE CHILD LEARNS SELF-CARE.—He should have in his own room, or in a corner of another's (if he has no room of his own) a tiny washstand, with a little bowl and pitcher, light enough for him to handle, and a mirror hung low enough for him to see if he has succeeded in getting his face clean. He should be allowed the time necessary to wash his face and hands, and should be taught to empty the bowl and to keep his washstand neat and clean. If this habit is begun at an early age, it is not at all difficult for a very young child to acquire it very thoroughly, and to be more conscientious about it, and similar matters of personal neatness, than many a half-grown boy or girl who have never been systematically trained. As soon as possible, he should be encouraged and allowed to dress himself, his clothes being made with this in view, although there must always be some buttons which three and four-year-old fingers cannot reach, and should assume the responsibility of putting away his own clothes and knowing where they are. People who have struggled with older children on these subjects will be surprised to note how naturally and easily a little child will assume these helpful and desirable habits. The important point is to "catch him young," before he has learned other bad habits of irresponsibility and sloth. Of course, there should be, as far as humanly possible, the greatest amount of regularity and routine in the little life. He should eat his meals at regular hours, feeding himself and sitting at a low table; he should take his naps regularly; he should always "pick up" his own room before leaving it in the morning, and do what small household tasks are his every day, without fail.

And this simple, industrious, tranquil life, with no excitements of joining in adult "pleasures"; full of profitable "play" which is educational, and permeated with a sense of responsibility on the child's part for the conduct of his own life, *is the Montessori life* for a child between two and seven. It is not enough that he construct the Tower, and the Long Stair, and learn his sandpaper letters perfectly; he must learn to be a self-dependent, self-respecting, self-trusting citizen of his little world.

EXERCISE TWENTY-THREE

FIRST STEPS IN ARITHMETIC

COUNTING BOXES AND SANDPAPER NUMBERS.—We have now to consider the question of arithmetic and the Montessori application of the subject to the child of the average American home. There is a prejudice in the minds of most Americans about presenting mathematics to children under six, no matter how simply it may be arranged. My own experience, backed up by that of the Casa dei Bambini, is that children over three take a lively interest in the sequence of numbers, and in some of the simpler processes of arithmetic, if those processes can be presented to them in a sufficiently concrete form. The Montessori apparatus for this purpose is very simple, and can be supplemented by several other devices, easily obtained in any home.

These counting boxes comprise two small boxes, with five compartments or divisions in each. Accompanying the two boxes are fifty smooth, round sticks, exactly alike, and a set of numbers from 0 to 9, cut out of sandpaper and pasted on white cards. The counting sticks give the child a concrete basis for the abstract names of the numbers, and he learns to associate the symbol with the concrete object. At first the child does not play with the sandpaper numbers. These are removed from the boxes and he but wrestles with the problem of oral counting, using the sticks. One good way to begin is by arranging one of the boxes as the illustration shows, the one to the left of the page, the numbers having been removed; that is, there are no sticks in the first compartment, one in the next, two in the next, three in the next, and four in the last. This exercise is, of course, for a very little child, who has no idea of the definite sequence of numbers, or of how to determine how many objects he holds in his hand. The other box is then emptied of all its contents and given the child, with an ample supply of the counting sticks, and he is invited to make his box exactly like the one his mother has arranged. Most children can, even at a very early age, quickly put one stick in the second compartment and two in the next. Here frequently, at the very beginning, there ensues some mental confusion, and much eager gazing at the three sticks in the box arranged by, the mother. Anxious attempts are made by the child to lay an equal number in the next compartment of his own box. The mother should not help in this process. It does the child no good if she interferes and does it herself, or corrects his mistake. If he has arrived at the age when his brain can master this simple arithmetical idea, he will ultimately solve the problem and place the proper number of sticks in each compartment. If he has not yet arrived at the right age or state of development, he will not really take in the significance of anything his mother may do, seeking to aid him. If he repeatedly performs this exercise incorrectly, or shows signs of mental fatigue, such as nervous irritation at his inability to solve the problem, the boxes should be removed, and the attempt postponed until a later day.

ASTONISHING MENTAL GROWTH. — The mental growth of children at this age is so astonishingly rapid that sometimes a child will be able easily to solve a problem only a week after he has found it perfectly impenetrable. It is quite possible that during the week some subconscious forces of the mind have been, quite unknown to the child, working on the problem presented. In no other way can an explanation be found of the surprising manner in which, after failing on a Montessori exercise, a child will take it up, several days later, without having touched it in the meantime, and know how to set to work purposefully and successfully. It is far better to trust this principle of growth than to attempt to urge the child to put forth powers which he does not as yet possess.

BEGINS TO COUNT.—As soon as he can complete the series up to four, he can go on, one at a time, to complete the series up to nine, as shown in the illustration; and then, if he is the normal child, with a wide-awake, intelligent, curious mind, he will be observed "counting" everything in sight. He is delighted with his new acquisition, and employs it on all the material at hand. A child of three and-a-half, who had just mastered the sequence in the counting boxes, ran about the house, counting the windows, the drawers in the bureaus, the chairs in the rooms, the legs of the tables, and deriving the most mysterious satisfaction, which lasted for many days, from this new control of the world about him. He gets, of course, from having his interest and own initiative once aroused, vastly more drill in repetition exercise than the most ingenious teacher could give him.

Children putting away Didactic material, National Kindergarten College, Chicago

EXERCISE TWENTY-FOUR

THE SANDPAPER NUMBERS ARE ADDED

Now is the time to bring out the sandpaper numbers. He is taught these just as he learned his letters, one at a time, and following the three regular steps. First, the mother guides the little forefinger over the rough sandpaper as the number would be written, at the same time pronouncing the name of the number, slowly and distinctly, and adding no explanations. She should here, as always, refrain from the wordy comments to which we are all too much given, and should not say, "See, this is 8. It looks like 'S,' only a little different; you see, S is open here, and here," etc. She should, instead, hold up the card, say clearly, "8," and show the little fingers how to trace the outline. Then she should lay several down on the table, and ask the child, "Give me '7,'" or, "Give me '2,' please." When he has mastered this, she should then hold up a card and ask the child to tell her what it is. When he can do this accurately, he has mastered his numbers. According to his age and capacity, this may take him two days, or two weeks. The next thing to do is to teach him to connect them with the right number of objects. And here the counting boxes come again into play. He should arrange the series, and place the right number in each compartment. The mother will be surprised to see that even after mastering the names and looks of the number and the sequence in the number boxes, the average child finds it quite an intellectual effort to put the two things together in his mind. He will need plenty of time and quiet to struggle with the new problem, and if it is too hard on the first trial, the number boxes should be taken away without comment, and some other "game" suggested.

EXERCISE TWENTY-FIVE

An Arithmetical Game with the Long Stair. —Another arithmetical game is played with the Long Stair. The stair is arranged in sequence and a cardboard number corresponding with the number of rods in the section is leaned up against the section; "1" against the section with only one rod, the "2" against the next one, and so forth. I remember seeing a child of four go slowly through this exercise in a Casa dei Bambini, taking frequent rests, but returning with a steady, purposeful industry to his undertaking, until he had the whole sequence up to ten correctly numbered. And then he lay down and took a brief nap, being apparently quite exhausted by the mental effort involved in what seems the simplest possible of rational connections between ideas.

A Game with Money.—About this time, or perhaps a little earlier, it is well to begin to teach a child the significance of money. He is always interested in this, seeing it of so much importance in the life of adults, and will play with it endlessly, and study the possible combinations to be made with it, if they are suggested to his mind. It is better, if possible, to have new money. If this cannot be managed, the coins should be thoroughly cleansed before the child plays with them. The mother should teach him the names of the different coins with the same three steps used in teaching him the names of the letters and numbers; that is, first tell him the names, slowly, one or two at a time; then ask him for a given coin; then point to a given coin and ask what it is called. At first the little child likes, as a rule, simply to sort out the money into the right piles, all the pennies together, all the nickels, all the quarters, etc. He should be allowed to play in this way until he is thoroughly acquainted with their names and sizes.

Then, if he is old enough to count with certainty up to ten, the relative value of the different coins can be explained to him; five pennies equal one nickel, etc. This is somewhat complicated, and care should be taken to go very slowly, only a little on any one day. When he has grasped something of this relation, the mother can hold up a nickel and ask, "How many pennies do I want for this?"

Or she and the child can play a simple version of the "going shopping" game, always so fascinating to older children. "I want six pennies for this spool of thread." "How much do you want for that doll?" etc.

ARITHMETICAL GAME WITH COUNTING STICKS.— An interesting "game" which can be played with numbers, if there are two or more children together, is the following: A certain number of the counting sticks, or any other objects such as clothespins, stones, spoons, coins, etc., are placed on a table. The mother then holds a bag containing the numbers up to ten. Each child draws a number at random, and, without showing it to his companions, goes back to his seat. When all have drawn their numbers, each child goes up to the table and selects from it the number of objects corresponding with the number hidden in his hand. He carries these back to his place and arranges them in order, and waits for the mother or teacher to come and verify the correctness of his counting.

TEACHES SELF-CONTROL.—This simple game, which would not amuse older children for a moment, is of inexhaustible interest for little ones, and has a various and complex influence on them. There is a considerable amount of self-control involved in their taking only the number of objects indicated by the number they have drawn, since every child's instinctive action is to grab all he can hold and carry off his prize in triumph. The mother should explain that this spoils the fun of the game, which consists in fitting the mysterious written sign to the number of objects chosen. Another conception which is firmly settled in the child's mind by this and other similar "games" is the abstract idea of "zero," since the child who draws zero selects no objects at all.

GAME WITH SANDPAPER NUMBERS. — Another arithmetical game which can be played with one or many children is played with the sandpaper numbers, or any large numbers, such as could be cut out of old calendars. The mother or teacher holds up a number and asks, "Come and give me this many kisses," or, "Bring me this number of pennies." This sort of "fun" familiarizes the mind of the little child with the connection between the written sign and the number, and especially fixes in his brain (in the game just described) the real concept of the sign "zero," which is often a stumblingblock to older children.

GAME WITH MOVABLE ALPHABET.—A similar game can be played with the movable alphabet, with older children, who have learned the beginnings of reading. The mother constructs a word, say for instance, "pin," and, pointing it out to the child, says, "Bring me this, please." The child who is first to read the word and select the article, wins. When several children of the same age and acquirements play this together, the fun, and intensity of interest, and consequent sharpening of wits, form an invaluable exercise.

HIDE-AND-SEEK WITH MOVABLE ALPHABET.—A game of hide-and-seek can also be played with children who have begun to recognize words formed with the movable alphabet. The mother constructs, in different parts of the room, different simple words which the child has already seen, such as "pig," "hen," "dog," etc. The child is out of the room while this is being done, and is called back to be told, "I hear something grunting." He then rushes about, peering under the chairs and on the table and window-sills, rejecting all other words he finds, until he comes triumphantly to "pig." It is better, with little children, to use the movable alphabet for these words, rather than writing them on paper, even in the plainest script, for two reasons: first, the child is more used to the movable alphabet; and second, the letters are so very large that there can be not the slightest opportunity for eye-strain.

EXERCISE TWENTY-SIX

THE MONTESSORI SILENCE TRAINING

There is one phase of the Montessori training which has not yet been touched upon, and it is rather hard to manage in the ordinary small American family. That is the exercise known as "Making the Silence." I quote the description of this impressive exercise, given in *A Montessori Mother,* so that the American mother may have some idea of what she is to try to imitate, in her differing circumstances:

"One may be moving about between the groups of busy children, or sitting watching their lively animation, or listening to the cheerful hum of their voices, when one feels a curious change in the atmosphere, like the hush which falls on a forest when the sun suddenly goes behind a cloud. If it is the first time that one has seen this "lesson," the effect is startling. A quick glance around shows that the children have stopped playing as well as talking, and are sitting motionless at their tables, their eyes on the blackboard, where, in large letters, is written, 'Silenzio' (Silence). Even the little ones, who cannot read, follow the example of the older ones and not only sit motionless but look fixedly at the magic word. The Directress is visible now, standing by the blackboard, in an attitude and with an expression of tranquillity which is as calming to see as the meditative impassivity of a Buddhist priest. The silence becomes more and more intense. To untrained ears it seems absolute, but an occasional gesture or warning smile from the Directress shows that a little hand has moved, almost but not quite inaudibly, or a chair has creaked.

"And then a real veil of twilight falls to intensify the effect. The Directress goes quietly about from window to window, closing the shutters. In the ensuing twilight, the children bow their heads on their clasped hands, in the attitude of prayer. The Directress steps through the door into the next room, and a slow voice, faint and clear, comes floating back, calling a child's name: 'El—e—na!'

"A child lifts her head, opens her eyes, rises as silently as a little spirit, and, with a glowing face of exaltation, tiptoes out of the room, flinging herself joyously into the waiting arms.

"The summons comes again, 'Vit—to—rio!'

"A little boy lifts his head from his desk, showing a face of sweet, sober content at being called, and goes silently across the big room, taking his place by the side of the Directress. And so it goes, until perhaps fifteen children are clustered happily about the teacher. Then, as informally and naturally as it began, the 'game' is over. The teacher comes back into the room with her usual quiet, firm step; light pours in at the windows; the mystic word is erased from the blackboard. The children smile at each other, and begin to play again, perhaps a little more quietly than before, perhaps more gently, certainly with the shining eyes of devout believers who have blessedly lost themselves in an instant of rapt and self-forgetting devotion.''

Now, this exercise is, of course, practically impossible to imitate exactly in a small family, but some adaptation of it should be made, for its benefits are too important to be missed. It was begun as an exercise for the sense of hearing, since the children are called in the lightest possible whisper; but it was soon seen to be of great moral importance. Such a period of perfect silence and immobility, if he takes it of his own accord, has the most miraculously calming effect on the average nervous, high-strung American child.

It can be begun by a laughing competition between mother and child, or between two or more children, to see who can ''keep the stillest.'' The one who moves first has ''lost.'' The mother can set the example by standing in the middle of the room, so intensely quiet that it is ''as if she were not there.'' Or she can sit beside the child on a bed or sofa, and try with him to be so silent that any one entering the room could not guess their presence. A slightly darkened room adds to the quieting effect of this exercise. Or she can leave him in a room by himself until he is perfectly silent, and then call him in a faint whisper, after which he tries to leave the room so silently that his footsteps cannot be heard.

GAMES THAT TEACH SELF-CONTROL AND COMMAND OF THE FIVE SENSES

An exercise in pure immobility can be given by showing the child his shadow, cast by a bright light back of him, and asking him if he can keep so quiet that his shadow will not quiver. The shadow is so much enlarged that the slightest motion is readily perceived by the child.

These exercises are taken because, to have perfect control of the muscles of the body, it is as essential to be able to do nothing with them as to be able to use them accurately. The ordinary children's game, like "blind-man's buff," where the players must be silent or they will be caught, are fine practice for attaining this capacity to sit or stand perfectly quiet, and children should be encouraged to play them. In fact, many of our homeliest and most familiar children's games are based on the pleasure children naturally take in learning self-control, and command of their five senses. "Hide-and-seek" in all its forms is fine exercise for little children, who often, at the beginning, find it impos-

sible to control themselves long enough to remain
hidden. And "hunt-the-thimble" is splendid practice for concentrating the naturally wandering attention of little ones. They should be taught these
games carefully, and some supervision given at first,
to make sure they have caught the idea, and then
every inducement given to continue playing them.

EXERCISE TWENTY-EIGHT

TURNING THE CHILD'S EVERYDAY ACTIVITIES INTO MONTESSORI EXERCISES

Before leaving the discussion of the formal Montessori apparatus and going on to the discussion
of the Montessori idea of obedience and discipline,
I wish to make one more general remark, to the
effect that the mother will do well to remember
that practically anything which the child takes into
its head to do (provided it is not injurious to himself or others) can be made into a more or less
efficient Montessori exercise, which will teach him
command of material objects and muscular self-
control. Restrain as much as possible the natural
instinct to cry to an inquiring, investigating three
or four-year-old child, "Don't touch that!" "Come
away from there!" etc. Of course, if he is trying
to reach a basin of boiling water, such peremptory
commands to inaction are necessary. But in most

cases a moment's reflection shows that the child's action is not "naughty" in itself, and if the action is directed in the right way, will harm neither himself nor the object touched. If he suddenly perceives the curious way in which drawers in a bureau open and shut, he should not be called away and forbidden to touch them. Our first thought is that he is trying to get at the contents of the drawer to injure them; whereas, in nine cases out of ten, his only interest is in mastering the mechanism of the sliding drawer. Now is the time, while his interest is aroused, to show him how to open and shut drawers easily, without drawing them out too far, without pinching his fingers when he shuts them up. This practical exercise in one of the processes of everyday life is quite as good as any "lesson" taught by the Montessori apparatus in a Casa dei Bambini. The child can do no possible harm by opening and shutting the drawers, and he is learning a very great deal about the way to manage his muscles and to concentrate his attention on the operation he undertakes.

ANALYZE THE CHILD'S MOTIVES.—There are, in the course of every day in an ordinary home, innumerable such exercises, which are forbidden the average child, simply because his parents do not take the trouble to analyze his needs. Of course, it will not do to allow a child to crumple up freshly ironed table linen, but we are mistaken in thinking that a little child had any "naughty" motive in doing this. His desire was to handle cloth, as he sees his mother handling it; to try to fold it up, and spread it out, and lay it evenly over a table or chair. An old dishcloth will do as well for him as one's best dinner napkin. In short, one should cultivate the habit of asking one's self definitely, before forbidding an action to a child, "Is it really bad for him to do it?" "Will he really injure anything by doing it?" and finally (this the most important), "Is there not some substitute activity which I could provide for him, without the objectionable features of what he is doing?"

How to Avoid Giving Negative Commands.— Every mother should have a fixed rule for herself, to give as few as possible merely negative commands. She should try almost never to say merely, "Don't do that," but to have the quick inventiveness to say, "You may now do this," or "You may not do that; but here is something very much like it which you *may* do."

EXERCISE TWENTY-NINE

LEARNING TO USE BOOKS AND TO HANDLE DELICATE AND FRAGILE OBJECTS

Instead of forbidding a little child to touch books, on the contrary, he should be given certain strongly bound, plain volumes, and allowed to handle them, after the method of treating them carefully has been explained to him—always in the Montessori manner of brief explanations and few words. Even very little children often show the greatest pleasure in "playing" with a book, turning over the leaves and pretending to read aloud, and their little fingers learn deft care in the use of printed pages, which makes it, as they grow older, no more natural for them than for an adult to tear or mutilate a volume.

They should be allowed an occasional exercise, granted as a great privilege, of handling and looking at some delicate objects, like embroidered table linen, or the contents of a jewel box. They will soon learn to wash their hands with fervor and to touch such fine and breakable objects with the most breathless care. How else can they learn properly to treat fragile objects, except by handling them once in a while? Of course, the concentration necessary for them to be careful and cautious in lifting and looking at such things is too great for them to continue at it very long. After a time, the box of doilies, or the fancy pins and rings, or the handsomely illustrated book, should be taken away and a less breakable or spoilable plaything given. But it is a great mistake to treat a child, even as young as three, as though he were maliciously destructive, and to have him, for instance, always eat from a tin plate and drink from a tin or silver cup. He will acquire inevitably the mental habit of carelessness in handling such objects. His tin cup will not break if he drops it—why should he take any pains *not* to drop it? The four-year-old children in Rome who bring in from the school kitchen big tureens of hot soup, and wash the dishes after a meal, successfully, should be remembered. The little child should be carefully trained, by the formal Montessori apparatus, to a firm, light, unhurried grasp on what he takes hold of, and then should be trusted with this new power.

Trust the Child.—The more he is trusted, the more astonished will be his mother at the extent to which it is quite safe to trust him. If he has not been forbidden always to touch things, there will be no temptation to furtive and disobedient handlings of objects, always with the fear of being discovered, which makes for nervousness and muscular uncertainty. The mother will find that a child who is allowed to learn by practicing the various household processes shows no desire to be the merely destructive force which so many older, untrained children helplessly show themselves.

If the child is provided with a goodly supply of objects to handle, there is little temptation to touch the few things which are rightly forbidden him. I know a nervous, active little girl of four, who is allowed to play freely with all the objects on her father's writing desk, with the single exception of the fountain pen and the ink, which are the only things she might injure. She has, at intervals, amused herself for six months with the other objects —the blotter pad and the calendar, the letter weight, the book rack, the letter basket—and never once, in all that time, has ever suggested touching the ink well, nor has ever forgotten to replace carefully the objects handled.

Treat the Child as Human Being.—In general, it should be remembered that the very little child, who has had no opportunity to acquire bad mental habits, is a member of the family and a human being, as much as any of the adults, and should be treated as such. He has no natural, inborn desire to destroy objects, if he can learn how to handle them without injuring them. He learns from touching, weighing, handling objects of different sizes and shapes, and he should be allowed to do this, unless there is a positive, serious reason against it.

Torresdale House, Torresdale, Phil. First building erected in America for Montessori work, at a cost of $30,000.00

The Junior Montessori Room, Torresdale House

V

SUGGESTIVE EXERCISES ON NATURE STUDY

Nature Study is one of the subjects which (owing to conditions in Rome) Dr. Montessori has not yet fully elaborated, so that whatever is done now in that direction by American mothers, using her principles with young children, must be largely the result of their own initiative. It will be well to read any good manual of Nature Study used in kindergarten and the lower grades; and the State Agricultural Experiment Stations of various states, notably that of Cornell University, have issued some suggestive pamphlets on the subject, which may be secured by sending a request.

However, any mother lucky enough to be bringing up her children in a small town or the country, with a few trees and a bit of ground available, needs only a jog to her inventiveness. The changing seasons will provide an illustrated history which needs only a running commentary to make it intelligible to the child.

Throughout this work, the mother should bear in mind the strong conviction of Dr. Montessori on

103

this subject. The Dottoressa holds that the usual pretty, fanciful, fairy-tale wording of information about facts of Nature is harmful and misleading to young children, who are quite literal-minded about accepting fairies and the like. For this reason, all kindergarten literature and nature study should be taken with a grain of salt on the mother's part. A maple leaf is not a fairy hand; a morning-glory is not a tent for the fairies; the buds of the trees in winter time are not "cradles" for leaves, but are the germs of leaves, protected from the cold, etc. The average child has naturally only too inaccurate a gaze at objects. He needs no encouragement to imagine them something different from what they are. If he is to have fairies, let him have them frankly imaginary, and not confuse with them the actual facts of the universe. The facts of nature, the growth of plants, seeds, etc., are quite wonderful and fantastic enough to interest any child without dressing them up in a wildly imaginary lingo which throws his simple mind entirely off the right track. I knew a child who had been told that the leaf-buds in winter were the cradles for the leaves, and who lost his entire faith in his teachers when a winter bud was cut open before him, and no leaf rolled out. It is hard to conceive the entire, literal faith of little children in what they are told. The greatest care should be taken not to abuse this by telling them things that are not so. Things that are so are more than interesting enough.

The growth of tree buds can be studied in the house by taking a small branch from a tree in January or February and letting it open in the warm air of an indoor room. This process takes place so slowly that every child whose attention is called to it, day after day, will have it firmly impressed upon his mind. The growth of seeds can be shown by planting close to the edge of an old jelly glass filled with earth. The growth of the young roots can be watched through the glass. A supply of small pots to grow different sorts of plants is also a good bit of "apparatus." The simplest varieties are the best—corn, peas, grass, etc. If this is done in winter, when there is not the bewildering variety of vegetation outdoors, the child—even the very young child—will soon come to recognize different plants very readily, and to have some notion of their requirements.

In summer time, a great deal is absorbed by simply living close to Mother Earth, especially if the parents are interested in processes of Nature. The child should have, if possible, a little garden of his own, which he is allowed to care for "all himself," and his attention should be called to the actions of ants, birds, insects, chickens, etc. He should then be allowed to observe these things, independent of supervision and suggestion, using them as he uses his Montessori apparatus, as a means to self-education. It is a good plan, if possible, to have drawn on large sheets of paper simple outlines of common birds and animals, which the child fills in with colors. Do not correct him if he makes a pig green, or the sky pink. The fact that he is thinking at all about the color of pigs and the sky will make him, some day, of his own accord, notice the real color, and this discovery will be of infinitely more value to him if he has made it quite himself. The difference between weeds (plants that are not useful) and flowers and vegetables should be explained to him, and his aid secured for the campaign against weeds. He is certain to feel a great self-importance at being allowed to help in the care of the garden.

VI

MONTESSORI GENERAL IDEAS ABOUT DISCIPLINE AND OBEDIENCE

The philosophy underlying all of the Montessori Method for educating young children was briefly described before the apparatus was taken up. No one should undertake to use the apparatus without a firm grasp on that master principle, that the aim of education in the case of the little child (as for all of us) is not the acquisition of knowledge, but the desire and capacity to acquire knowledge; and further, that since the child must himself feel and acquire this desire and this capacity, it is essential to leave him as much opportunity as possible for the exercise of his own initiative and his own invention. For the three-year-old, as for the ten-year-old, it will do the child no good for the mother to learn his lessons for him. The joy of a little child's heart is in overcoming obstacles, and if his mother takes all the obstacles away from him, she takes the flavor out of his life. The Montessori apparatus—the whole Montessori idea—is meant to furnish appropriate obstacles for children of three and four, and five and six years old.

Since this general philosophy was stated at the beginning of this Manual, there is no necessity for repeating that statement here. But there is one phase of the Montessori idea which needs more explicit expression than it is apt to get in general descriptions of the system. That is the question of discipline and obedience. Those two subjects are so vital and so tragically misunderstood by most of us, that it may be well to go a little more deeply into the discussion of them.

INTELLIGENT OBEDIENCE.—The first thing to do, in the consideration of the obedience of children, is to differentiate clearly in our minds between the obedience that is desirable for an animal, and that which is desirable for the young of the human race. We are apt to be confused here, and to have a misunderstood notion that children should obey, unquestioningly, passively, with no volition of their own, as does a well-broken horse. But such unquestioning obedience, as a moment's reflection will show, is a very dangerous mental habit for a child to acquire, as well as a very difficult one to force him to acquire. The horse may obey unquestioningly some human being; he will always have some human being set in authority over him. But in a very few years, as human life goes, the child will be grown; will no longer be subject to the authority of parents, and must in turn be able to secure the obedience of others. It is essential, therefore, that he shall begin to be a human being—that is, to obey intelligently —as soon as possible. What do we mean by the phrase "obey intelligently?" We mean he must obey, not because some one has told him to and will punish him if he does not, for that is the obedience exacted of the animal; but he will obey because the command is a reasonable one, which his reason tells him it is necessary to obey. We adults do not refrain from robbing and murdering and burning down other people's houses simply because we are afraid a policeman will arrest us if we do. We refrain from doing such things because we are law-abiding American citizens. Let us help to make our children law-abiding American citizens, and not the victims of Russian irrational tyranny.

THE BASIS OF PARENTS' AUTHORITY.—Our children should understand that their duty is *not* to obey our *personal wishes,* because we happen to be their parents, but to obey eternal laws which we represent and expound and enforce. To take an instance, familiar to all of us, which comes into our everyday experience: Children should not, any more than they can help, be "messy" over their meals; should not spill food on the tablecloth, or on their clothes, or be unpleasant in their way of eating. Why should they not do these things? Simply because their parents forbid it? Not at all. Because it is their duty, as members of a community, to make the common life as agreeable, as easy, and as economically conducted as possible. Their parents' duty is not at all to cry, "You do it because I say so!" but to explain reasonably the underlying grounds of conduct, to allow a reasonable time for an understanding of the principle to reach the child's brain, and then to be unflinching in their police duty of enforcing obedience—obedience *not to themselves,* but to a law, which they must obey as well as the children. If there is no such general broad basis for a command given to a child, it is an unjust command, and should not be issued. *No child should be forced to obey a whim of the parent,* but only, some modification of one of the general laws which he will need to obey when he is grown up.

THE MANAGEMENT OF THE VERY YOUNG CHILD OF UNREASONING AGE.—Now, of course, it is impossible for very little children to make this distinction. Babies under eighteen months must be forced to obey, if the occasion rises, as other little unreasonable animals are forced, by sheer physical compulsion. But, as this is a very bad method of obtaining obedience, the occasions for requiring obedience should be sedulously avoided, as much as is reasonably possible, during this animal-like period of the child's growth. No one thinks of requiring obedience of a week-old baby, and yet he is in many respects just as capable of being obedient as many a year-old child. If you need to move a week-old baby from one spot to another, you do not stand off and command him to move—you pick him up and carry him; and the same treatment is often best for the irrational year-old baby.

PARENTS UNCONSCIOUSLY FORCE CHILDREN TO DISOBEDIENCE.—Parents, in their great anxiety to avoid that utter abomination, a disobedient child, often are entirely unreasonable in their demands on very young children. You would not dream of asking your two-year-old son to do a sum in arithmetic; and yet you tell him peremptorily to do that far harder thing, "Do keep still for a minute!" He *cannot* keep still for a minute at that age, and to issue that command to him means simply that you yourself are initiating him into the meaning of disobedience. In general, then, with very young children, the method of procedure should be:

First.—To so arrange his life that there shall be few needs to issue commands. A child who is kept quietly at home, playing with objects designed for his use, who is not "shown off" to adults, who is not forced into such cruel situations as enforced participation in adult life, like traveling on the cars, going to church, or to shops, or on the street cars, or asked to entertain a company of idle elders, will rarely be insubordinate, or think of such a thing as disobeying, for the simple reason that the things asked of him are within his capacity to do. On the rare occasion when such a crisis arises, it is best frankly to treat the little creature like a speechless animal, which he is, and enforce obedience to something necessary. But this should, in any ordinary normal child's life, happen not more than once or twice up to his second year.

Second.—As soon as he begins to be able to understand simple statements, the reason for various commands given him should be explained to him. One result of this rule is apt to be that fewer commands are given, as they are often seen to rest upon utterly unreasonable grounds. The child should be trained, first, to obey promptly, and then to expect an explanation of the action. In most cases this careful clarifying in his mind of the grounds for action, results in a most satisfactory régime of reasonableness. Suppose, for instance, that a child is seen climbing upon a chair before the sideboard in the dining-room. His mother should not call out to him simply, "Come away from there!" but should explain to him that it is dangerous for him to handle the glasses, standing in rows on the top, because he would be apt to break them. If the child then asks to be allowed to play with the spoons in the drawer, there is no reasonable grounds for refusing that request. He has made a concession, and has learned self-control and obedience in refraining from touching the glasses, and his mother has, if she is alert-minded enough to learn a lesson, taken note that her command, "Come away from there!" was not exactly fitted to the case. She should have analyzed the situation more acutely, and see that she need not forbid a harmless amusement to the child because it happened to be in proximity to a potentially harmful one. Such frank explanation and mutual concession are most valuable and vital elements in the harmonious relations of parent and child, and do more than anything else to prevent that bitter rebellion against authority which so often saddens the adolescence of children with strong wills and a keen sense of justice.

Third.—The mother should make the most careful distinction between the conscious, willful action of a child, and the sort of wild irritability which results in "naughty" actions, but which is the result itself of nervous fatigue, due to injudicious treatment. In the Casa dei Bambini, on the very rare occasions when a child is "naughty," he is treated as a "sick" child; is put off in a quiet corner of the room, allowed all the toys he wishes to play with, is soothed and petted, allowed everything but (this is the important point) to play with the other children. In a short time this reduces the most unruly child to submission. But in an ordinary home, with only two or three children, the "naughty" child is not privileged, like the Italian child in the Montessori school, to see constantly before him the precious example of the orderly, peaceable, industrious behavior of thirty other children. The principle, however, holds. Nine times out of ten, the "naughty" child *is,* in all sober reality, a sick child, or at least a very tired child. It is hard for adults to realize what a nervous strain it is, for instance, for a child of three to see strange faces for a few hours. I have known several cases of children, even as old as four and five, who were reduced to what was practically nervous hysteria by a trip down town with an adult, going in the street cars, and being taken to several shops. The mothers of these children were in despair over their naughty and turbulent dispositions, as no amount of disciplining did the least good. Of course, it did not. The child's sensitive nerves were, for the time being, in such a tense, unnatural state of strain that the child, for all practical purposes, was insane. When another régime was adopted, of unvarying quiet for the child, of a tranquil, peaceful routine, *never* changed, with few persons in it, and plenty of sleep, regularly taken, the "naughty" dispositions vanished like magic, and sweet-tempered, loving, tractable little children proved that the trouble had been purely physical and nervous.

Now, this means in many ways quite a sacrifice on the part of the mother. In most cases, if she cannot take the children with her, on shopping and pleasure excursions, she is obliged to stay at home with them. Sometimes, however, even where there is no grandmother or aunt who can be left for a few hours with the little ones, an arrangement can be made with a neighbor who also has little children, to "trade" with her, to take care of her children as well as your own for one afternoon, on condition that she do the same for you. If neither of these are possible, then the mother, if she is conscientious and really wishes to do the best possible for her children, must simply resign herself to a very quiet life during their early childhood. She can reflect that she may expect, under ordinary circumstances, to live to be seventy or more years old, and that to give up five or even eight years of all that time to the care of her little children is not a large proportion of her life. And she will be more than repaid, in the ease of "managing" her children, if she can secure for them a perfectly regular, even, tranquil life, with absolutely no adult excitements. She should keep before her mind the perfectly happy, perfectly good children in the Roman Casa dei Bambini, who never, never, have a change, who know no other life than the round of work and fun which is specially adapted to them.

If such a régime is rigorously adhered to, in the ordinary family, ninety-nine per cent of the difficulty of disciplining little children would be entirely obviated. They learn to obey unconsciously, because they are never asked to exercise their will-power and self-control, when their sensitive little nerves are at the breaking point from fatigue and excitement. It is, of course, impossible absolutely to attain this ideal in the ordinary American family. There are sure to be cousins, and aunts, and uncles, and even grandmothers and grandfathers, little in sympathy with this rational and merciful method of treating little children—people who consider that part of a child's duty is to amuse and entertain its elders—people who say, "Oh, what's the good of having a child, if you can't have fun with it?" They are the sort of people who, fifteen years ago, used to insist upon tossing up and down a new-born baby, shaking bright-colored objects before its eyes, and generally driving it to nervous prostration; whereupon they left the house, and the parents were obliged to nurse the child over the almost inevitable fit of indigestion and "nerves" which followed. Such people now are the ones who like to make a three-year-old child "show off" and say "funny things." They still leave the parents to bear the brunt of the ensuing nervous attack.

SHOULD NOT DISCIPLINE OR TRY TO REASON WITH A CHILD WHEN NERVOUSLY EXCITED.—The only thing the mother can do in such a case is to remember that the child is not himself when nervously excited. There is no use trying to "reason" with him, or to discipline him, or arouse his better nature. For the moment he *has* no better nature! He is nothing but jangled nerves. A tired or excited young child should never be asked to exercise self-control; there should be no occasion for it. The only thing to do with him is to quiet him as soon as possible by purely physical means. If he is hungry, get him something, very easily digested, to eat; slip off his clothing, give him a warm bath, if possible, and lay him down in a comfortable bed, in a room not too light, with *plenty* of fresh air. When he has slept and rested, he will have "come to himself," and the necessity for punishment will be past. He will, as he always does when he is in good physical condition, *desire* to be a good child. There will be something there for the mother to work with. Even if he has had no special excitement, there may be times, in the life of an especially nervous child, when his vitality is at a low ebb, and the regular routine of life is too much for him. If he shows signs of nervous irritability, snarling and snapping, or crying at nothing, he should never be reproved.

He should be put to bed, not at all as a punishment, but with the tenderest affection and the most solemn pity for the poor little sensitive creature. If there is in this prescription of rest for nervous fret, no hint of punishment, or shame, the child will not resent it, but will soon learn to yield himself up to the soothing influence.

How to Avoid a "Brain-Storm."—If, when several little children are playing together, the mother hears one begin to speak in a loud, excited voice, and to have nervous, disorganized motions, such as knocking the playthings about, she should come up quietly to the group and remark calmly that "Johnny is evidently too tired to play any longer. He'd better go and rest for a time, until he feels better." Then he is led away, very gently. There should be the utmost care not to seem to use this as a chastisement. His face and hands should be washed in cool water (there is very apt to be a slight fever present when nervous irritability sets in), his clothing loosened, and he himself laid on a bed in a quiet room. This treatment has, in addition to the invaluable physical effect, a very strong moral one. The gentleness, the peace of the room, the utter isolation, the inaction—there seems nothing left for the child to battle with, nothing for his "naughtiness" to feed upon. In families where this humane régime is in force, I have

known instances of children of four and five, who
have begun to be self conscious and reasonable, who
come to their mothers and *ask* to be put to bed for
half an hour, because they "are beginning to feel
naughty." Children do not enjoy the miserable,
unhappy excitement of being naughty, no matter
what our misunderstanding reading of them may
seem to indicate. And if they have had a fair
experience of a sure escape from the "brain-storm"
of a fit of insubordination, they are very apt to
resort to it of their own accord. If it is evident
that the child cannot be sleepy, for instance, only
a short time after a nap, another calming expedi-
ent is to take him gently away from the others to
a quiet place outdoors, where he is left to play in
solitary proximity to the bosom of Mother Earth.

But of course this remedy cannot be applied, if
the nervous fit comes on while the mother is pric-
ing laces in a department store and the child hang-
ing to her skirts, or if they are at an "amusement
park," with bands braying and tooting about them,
and crowds of excited pleasure seekers noisily
going their way.

This is another reason for never taking children
away from the quiet home life, except to some
equally quiet spot out-of-doors.

This rule may be relaxed, of course, as the children grow older, but it should be relaxed very

gradually, with the fewest possible breaks in the tranquil and unchanging life.

Fourth.—NECESSITY FOR CONSTANT ACTIVITY IN EARLY CHILDHOOD.—The final lesson we American mothers have to learn from Dr. Montessori and her wonderful success with the training of little children, is the lesson of positiveness, as opposed to negativeness in their lives. The craving for constant, unceasing activity in little children is intense. This is a normal and blessed instinct of theirs, which does more than anything to develop them. And the mother should constantly bear it in mind. Her attitude towards her little child should be as little negative as may be; she should set her grown-up wits incessantly to work to devise wise, harmless and beneficial actions for the child, not merely to forbid him unwise and harmful ones. And here the Montessori apparatus is of incalculable value. It caters with scientific ingenuity to the need for action of the small child, and relieves the mother's inexperienced brain of a great part of the strain of inventing suitable exercises for children under six or seven. The child can be, to a large extent, turned loose with the Montessori apparatus, with the certainty that he will not hurt himself or anything else, and that he is learning something.

MONTESSORI APPARATUS NOT ENOUGH.—But the

Montessori apparatus, valuable as it is, is not enough. As has been said many times in the preceding pages, the mother's mind must be alert and ingenious to supplement it as the child grows. For instance, blunt pointed scissors and plenty of paper to cut are as indispensable as the geometric insets. Constant exercises in the occupations of every-day life, such as washing and wiping toy dishes and setting a small table, sweeping the floor with a small broom, learning to dust, etc., are as necessary as the sandpaper letters. If the children are initiated into these exercises young enough, before their natural instinct for action and for helpful action has been atrophied by the customary idling in early childhood, the mother will find the utmost eagerness for such activities, and not at all the lazy, shirking attitude towards them so frequently seen in older children, who did not have proper training in their early life.

HABIT OF OBEDIENCE A SLOW GROWTH.—Does all this seem a long way from the question of obedience? It is not in the least. For the question of obedience in the young children is largely concerned with other matters than obedience, or to put it differently, with indirect means of attaining obedience. Obedience for the moment can always be attained directly by the brutal method of using force, because the adult is always stronger than the little child. But, of course, obedience of this sort lasts exactly as long as the force can and is applied, which means an ungoverned adolescence for the child, and a childhood full of anger and storms of rebellion.

The other kind of obedience, the right kind, can be attained only very gradually, for it is at least as difficult an achievement as learning the multiplication table. The child needs to begin with very small beginnings in this as in any other important activity of his life, to be asked in early childhood to obey as seldom as possible, because his life is rightly and carefully suited to his needs; to have the reason for obedience; the real, underlying philosophic reason explained to him as soon as possible and as often as necessary; never to be asked or expected to obey when he is having what amounts to a fit of hysteria; and, finally, to have his life so filled with interesting, profitable and entertaining occupations that the question of obedience enters into it very little. Through the daily experience of living a well-ordered, industrious, purposeful life, he learns, unconsciously the joys of peace and tranquillity, and he comes to be as unwilling to wreck these by insubordination as his mother is unwilling to have him. Like any other good *habit,* obedience cannot come from one or two violent efforts. It must come from a long, long continuance in the right conditions. And to secure these "right conditions" the Montessori apparatus, method and philosophy are the most potent means as yet discovered.

VII

SOME OF THE QUESTIONS THAT ARE ANSWERED

ABOUT OBEDIENCE AND HOW IT IS OBTAINED

ABOUT DIDACTIC MATERIALS

INDEX TO MONTESSORI MANUAL